THE DELICIOUS VICE

Pipe Dreams and Fond Adventures of an Habitual
Novel-Reader Among Some Great Books and Their
People

Young E. Allison

1st WORLD
LIBRARY
Literary Society

The Delicious Vice

Young E. Allison

© 1st World Library – Literary Society, 2004
PO Box 2211
Fairfield, IA 52556
www.1stworldlibrary.org
First Edition

LCCN: 2004195370

Softcover ISBN: 1-59540-809-6
Hardcover ISBN: 1-59540-804-5
ebook ISBN: 1-59540-814-2

Purchase *"The Delicious Vice"*
as a traditional bound book at:
www.1stWorldLibrary.org/purchase.asp?ISBN=1-59540-809-6

1st World Library Literary Society is a nonprofit
organization dedicated to promoting literacy by:

- Creating a free internet library accessible from any
  computer worldwide.
- Hosting writing competitions and offering book
  publishing scholarships.

Readers interested in supporting literacy
through sponsorship, donations or
membership please contact:
literacy@1stworldlibrary.org
Check us out at: www.1stworldlibrary.ORG
and start downloading free ebooks today.

The Delicious Vice
contributed by Tim, Ed & Rodney
in support of
1st World Library Literary Society

I.

A RHAPSODY ON THE NOBLE PROFESSION OF NOVEL READING

It must have been at about the good-bye age of forty that Thomas Moore, that choleric and pompous yet genial little Irish gentleman, turned a sigh into good marketable "copy" for Grub Street and with shrewd economy got two full pecuniary bites out of one melancholy apple of reflection:

"Kind friends around me fall
Like leaves in wintry weather,"

- he sang of his own dead heart in the stilly night.

"Thus kindly I scatter thy leaves on the bed
Where thy mates of the garden lie scentless and dead."

- he sang to the dying rose. In the red month of October the rose is forty years old, as roses go. How small the world has grown to a man of forty, if he has put his eyes, his ears and his brain to the uses for which they are adapted. And as for time - why, it is no longer than a kite string. At about the age of forty everything that can happen to a man, death excepted, has happened; happiness has gone to the devil or is a mere habit; the blessing of poverty has been permanently secured or you are exhausted with the cares of wealth; you can see around the corner or you do not care to see around it; in a word - that is, considering mental existence - the bell has rung on you and you are up against a steady grind for the remainder of your life. It is then there comes to the habitual novel reader the inevitable day when, in anguish of heart, looking back over his life, he - wishes he hadn't; then he asks himself the bitter question if there are not things he has done that he wishes he hadn't. Melancholy marks him for its own. He sits in his room some winter evening, the lamp swarming shadowy seductions, the grate glowing with siren invitation, the cigar box within easy reach for that moment when the pending sacrifice between his teeth shall be burned out; his feet upon the familiar corner of the mantel at that automatically calculated altitude which permits the weight of the upper part of the body to fall exactly upon the second joint from the lower end of the vertebral column as it rests in the comfortable depression created by continuous wear in the cushion of that particular chair to which every honest man who has acquired the library vice sooner or later gets attached with a love no misfortune can destroy. As he sits thus, having closed the lids of, say, some old favorite of his youth, he will inevitably ask himself if it would not have been better for him if he hadn't. And the question once asked must be answered; and it will be an honest answer, too. For no scoundrel was ever addicted to the delicious vice of novel-reading. It is too tame for him. "There is no money in it."

*   *   *   *   *

And every habitual novel-reader will answer that

question he has asked himself, after a sigh. A sigh that will echo from the tropic deserted island of Juan Fernandez to that utmost ice-bound point of Siberia where by chance or destiny the seven nails in the sole of a certain mysterious person's shoe, in the month of October, 1831, formed a cross - thus:

```
       *
   *   *   *
       *
       *
       *
```

while on the American promontory opposite, "a young and handsome woman replied to the man's despairing gesture by silently pointing to heaven." The Wandering Jew may be gone, but the theater of that appalling prologue still exists unchanged. That sigh will penetrate the gloomy cell of the Abbe Faria, the frightful dungeons of the Inquisition, the gilded halls of Vanity Fair, the deep forests of Brahmin and fakir, the jousting list, the audience halls and the petits cabinets of kings of France, sound over the trackless and storm-beaten ocean - will echo, in short, wherever warm blood has jumped in the veins of honest men and wherever vice has sooner or later been stretched groveling in the dust at the feet of triumphant virtue.

And so, sighing to the uttermost ends of the earth, the old novel-reader will confess that he wishes he hadn't. Had not read all those novels that troop through his memory. Because, if he hadn't - and it is the impossibility of the alternative that chills his soul with the despair of cruel realization - if he hadn't, you see, he could begin at the very first, right then and there, and read the whole blessed business through for the first time. For the FIRST TIME, mark you! Is there anywhere in this great round world a novel reader of true genius who would not do that with the joy of a child and the thankfulness of a sage?

Such a dream would be the foundation of the story of a really noble Dr. Faustus. How contemptible is the man who, having staked his life freely upon a career, whines at the close and begs for another chance; just one more - and a different career! It is no more than Mr. Jack Hamlin, a friend from Calaveras County, California, would call "the baby act," or his compeer, Mr. John Oakhurst, would denominate "a squeal." How glorious, on the other hand, is the man who has spent his life in his own way, and, at its eventide, waves his hand to the sinking sun and cries out: "Goodbye; but if I could do so, I should be glad to go over it all again with you - just as it was!" If honesty is rated in heaven as we have been taught to believe, depend upon it the novel-reader who sighs to eat the apple he has just devoured, will have no trouble hereafter.

What a great flutter was created a few years ago when a blind multi-millionaire of New York offered to pay a million dollars in cash to any scientist, savant or surgeon in the world who would restore his sight. Of course he would! It was no price at all to offer for the service - considering the millions remaining. It was no more to him than it would be to me to offer ten dollars for a peep at Paradise. Poor as I am I will give any man in the world one hundred dollars in cash who will enable me to remove every trace of memory of M. Alexandre Dumas' "Three Guardsmen," so that I may open that glorious book with the virgin capacity of youth to enjoy its full delight. More; I will duplicate the same offer for any one or all of the following:

"Les Miserables," of M. Hugo.

"Don Quixote," of Senor Cervantes.

"Vanity Fair," of Mr. Thackeray.

"David Copperfield," of Mr. Dickens.

"The Cloister and the Hearth," of Mr. Reade.

And if my good friend, Isaac of York, is lending money at the old stand and will take pianos, pictures, furniture, dress suits and plain household plate as collateral, upon even moderate valuation, I will go fifty dollars each upon the following:

"The Count of Monte Cristo," of M. Dumas.

"The Wandering Jew," of M. Sue.

"The Memoirs of Barry Lyndon, Esq.," of Mr. Thackeray.

"Treasure Island," of Mr. Robbie Stevenson.

"The Vicar of Wakefield," of Mr. Goldsmith.

"Pere Goriot," of M. de Balzac.

"Ivanhoe," of Baronet Scott.

(Any one previously unnamed of the whole layout of M. Dumas, excepting only a paretic volume entitled "The Conspirators.")

Now, the man who can do the trick for one novel can do it for all - and there's a thousand dollars waiting to be earned, and a blessing also. It's a bald "bluff," of course, because it can't be done as we all know. I might offer a million with safety. If it ever could have been done the noble intellectual aristocracy of novel-readers would have been reduced to a condition of penury and distress centuries ago.

For, who can put fetters upon even the smallest second of eternity? Who can repeat a joy or duplicate a sweet sorrow? Who has ever had more than one first sweetheart, or more than one first kiss under the honeysuckle? Or has ever seen his name in print for the first time, ever again? Is it any wonder that all these inexplicable longings, these hopeless hopes, were summed up in the heart-cry of Faust -

"Stay, yet awhile, O moment of beauty."

*   *   *   *   *

Yet, I maintain, Dr. Faustus was a weak creature. He begged to be given another and wholly different chance to linger with beauty. How much nobler the magnificent courage of the veteran novel-reader, who in the old age of his service, asks only that he may be permitted to do again all that he has done, blindly, humbly, loyally, as before.

Don't I know? Have I not been there? It is no child's play, the life of a man who - paraphrasing the language of Spartacus, the much neglected hero of the ages - has met upon the printed page every shape of perilous adventure and dangerous character that the broad empire of fiction could furnish, and never yet lowered his arm. Believe me it is no carpet duty to have served on the British privateers in Guiana, under Commodore Kingsley, alongside of Salvation Yeo; to have been a loyal member of Thuggee and cast the scarf for Bowanee; to have watched the tortures of Beatrice Cenci (pronounced as written in honest English, and I spit upon the weaklings of the service who imagine that any freak of woman called Bee-ah-treech-y Chonchy could have endured the agonies related of that sainted lady) - to have watched those tortures, I say, without breaking down; to have fought under the walls of Acre with Richard Coeur de Lion; to have crawled, amid rats and noxious vapors, with Jean Valjean through the sewers of Paris; to have dragged weary miles through the snow with Uncas, Chief of the Mohicans; to have lived among wild beasts with Morok the lion tamer; to have charged with the impis of Umslopogaas; to have sailed before the mast with Vanderdecken, spent fourteen gloomy years in the next cell to Edmund Dantes, ferreted out the murders in the Rue Morgue, advised Monsieur Le Cocq and given years of life's prime in tedious professional assistance to that anointed idiot and pestiferous scoundrel, Tittlebat Titmouse! Equally, of course, it has not been all horror and despair. Life averages up fairly, as any novel-reader will admit, and there has been much of delight - even luxury and idleness - between the carnage hours of battle. Is it not so? Ask that boyish-hearted old scamp whom you have seen scuttling away from the circulating library with M. St. Pierre's memoirs of young Paul and his beloved Virginia under his arm; or stepping briskly out of the book store hugging to his left side a carefully wrapped biography of Lady Diana Vernon, Mlle. de la Valliere, or Madame Margaret Woffington; or in fact any of a thousand charming ladies whom it is certain he had met before. Ladies too, who, born whensoever, are not one day older since he last saw them. Nearly a hundred years of Parisian residence have not served to induce the Princess Haydee of Yanina to forego her picturesque Greek gowns and coiffures, or to alter the somewhat embarrassing status of her relations with her striking but gloomy protector, the Count of Monte Cristo.

The old memories are crowded with pleasures. Those delicious mornings in the allee of the park, where you were permitted to see Cosette with her old grandfather, M. Fauchelevent; those hours of sweet pain when it was impossible to determine whether it was Rebecca or Rowena who seemed to give most light to the day; the flirtations with Blanche Amory, and the notes placed in the hollow tree; the idyllic devotion of Little Emily, dating from the morning when you saw her dress fluttering on the beam as she ran along it, lightly, above the flowing tide - (devotion that is yet tender, for, God forgive you Steerforth as I do, you could not smirch that pure heart;) the melancholy, yet sweet sorrow, with which you saw the loved and lost Little Eva borne to her grave over which the mocking-bird now sings his liquid requiem. Has it not been sweet good fortune to love Maggie Tulliver, Margot of Savoy, Dora Spenlow (undeclared because she was an honest wife - even though of a most conceited and commonplace jackass, totally undeserving of her); Agnes Wicklow (a passion quickly cured when she took Dora's pitiful leavings), and poor ill-fated Marie Antoinette? You can name dozens if you have been brought up in good literary society.

* * * * *

These love affairs may be owned freely, as being perfectly honorable, even if hopeless. And, of course, there have been gallantries - mere affaires du jour - such as every man occasionally engages in. Sometimes they seemed serious, but only for a moment. There was Beatrix Esmond, for whom I could certainly have challenged His Grace of Hamilton, had not Lord Mohun done the work for me. Wandering down the street in London one night, in a moment of weak admiration for her unrivalled nerve and aplomb, I was hesitating - whether to call on Mrs. Rawdon Crawley, knowing that her thick-headed husband was in hoc for debt - when the door of her house crashed open and that old scoundrel, Lord Steyne, came wildly down the steps, his livid face blood-streaked, his topcoat on his arm and a dreadful look in his eye. The world knows the rest as I learned it half an hour later at the green-grocer's, where the Crawleys owed an inexcusably large bill. Then the Duchess de Langeais - but all this is really private.

After all, a man never truly loves but once. And somewhere in Scotland there is a mound above the gentle, tender and heroic Helen Mar, where lies buried the first love of my soul. That mound, O lovely and loyal Helen, was watered by the first blinding and unselfish tears that ever sprang from my eyes. You were my first love; others may come and inevitably they go, but you are still here, under the pencil pocket of my waistcoat.

Who can write in such a state? It is only fair to take a rest and brace up.

II

NOVEL-READERS AS DISTINGUISHED FROM WOMEN AND NIBBLERS AND AMATEURS

There is, of course, but one sort of novel-reader who is of any importance He is the man who began under the age of fourteen and is still sticking to it - at whatever age he may be - and full of a terrifying anxiety lest he may be called away in the midst of preliminary announcements of some pet author's "next forth-coming." For my own part I cannot conceive dying with resignation knowing that the publishers were binding up at the time anything of Henryk Sienckiewicz's or Thomas Hardy's. So it is important that a man begin early, because he will have to quit all too soon.

There are no women novel-readers. There are women who read novels, of course; but it is a far cry from reading novels to being a novel-reader. It is not in the nature of a woman. The crown of woman's character is her devotion, which incarnate delicacy and tenderness exalt into perfect beauty of sacrifice. Those qualities could no more live amid the clashings of indiscriminate human passions than a butterfly wing could go between the mill rollers untorn. Women utterly refuse to go on with a book if the subject goes against their settled opinions. They despise a novel - howsoever fine and stirring it may be - if there is any taint of unhappiness to the favorite at the close. But the most flagrant of all their incapacities in respect to fiction is the inability to appreciate the admirable achievements of heroes, unless the achievements are solely in behalf of women. And even in that event they complacently consider them to be a matter of course, and attach no particular importance to the perils or the hardships undergone. "Why shouldn't he?" they argue, with triumphant trust in ideals; "surely he loved her!"

There are many women who nibble at novels as they nibble at luncheon - there are also some hearty eaters; but 98 per cent of them detest Thackeray and refuse resolutely to open a second book of Robert Louis Stevenson. They scent an enemy of the sex in Thackeray, who never seems to be in earnest, and whose indignant sarcasm and melancholy truthfulness they shrink from. "It's only a story, anyhow," they argue again; "he might, at least write a pleasant one, instead of bringing in all sorts of disagreeable people - some of them positively disreputable." As for Stevenson, whom men read with the thrill of boyhood rising new in their veins, I believe in my soul women would tear leaves out of his novels to tie over the tops of preserve jars, and never dream of the sacrilege.

Now I hold Thackeray and Stevenson to be the absolute test of capacity for earnest novel-reading. Neither cares a snap of his fingers for anybody's prejudices, but goes the way of stern truth by the light of genius that shines within him.

If you could ever pin a woman down to tell you what she thought, instead of telling you what she thinks it is proper to tell you, or what she thinks will please you,

you would find she has a religious conviction that Dot Perrybingle in "The Cricket of the Hearth," and Ouida's Lord Chandos were actually a materializable an and a reasonable gentleman, either of whom might be met with anywhere in their proper circles, I would be willing to stand trial for perjury on the statement that I've known admirable women - far above the average, really showing signs of moral discrimination - who have sniveled pitifully over Nancy Sykes and sniffed scornfully at Mrs. Tess Durbeyfield Clare. It is due to their constitution and social heredity. Women do not strive and yearn and stalk abroad for the glorious pot of intellectual gold at the end of the rainbow; they pick and choose and, having chosen, sit down straightway and become content. And a state of contentment is an abomination in the sight of man. Contentment is to be sought for by great masculine minds only with the purpose of being sure never quite to find it.

* * * * *

For all practical purposes, therefore - except perhaps as object lessons of "the incorrect method" in reading novels - women, as novel-readers, must be considered as not existing. And, of course, no offense is intended. But if there be any weak-kneed readers who prefer the gilt-wash of pretty politeness to the solid gold of truth, let them understand that I am not to be frightened away from plain facts by any charge of bad manners.

On the contrary, now that this disagreeable interruption has been forced upon me - certainly not through any seeking of mine - it may be better to speak out and settle the matter. Men who have the happiness of being in the married state know that nothing is to be gained by failing to settle instantly with women who contradict and oppose them. Who was that mellow philosopher in one of Trollope's tiresomely clever novels who said: "My word for it, John, a husband ought not to take a cane to his wife too soon. He should fairly wait till they are half-way home from the church - but not longer, not longer." Of course every man with a spark of intelligence and gallantry wishes that women COULD rise to real novel-reading Think what courtship would be! Every true man wishes to heaven there was nothing more to be said against women than that they are not novel-readers. But can mere forgetting remove the canker? Do not all of us know that the abstract good of the very existence of woman is itself open to grave doubt - with no immediate hope of clearing up? Woman has certainly been thrust upon us. Is there any scrap of record to show that Adam asked for her? He was doing very well, was happy, prosperous and healthy. There was no certainty that her creation was one of that unquestionably wonderful series that occupied the six great days. We cannot conceal that her creation caused a great pain in Adam's side - undoubtedly the left side, in the region of the heart. She has been described by young and dauntless poets as "God's best afterthought;" but, now, really - and I advance the suggestion with no intention to be brutal but solely as a conscientious duty to the ascertainment of truth - why is it, that -. But let me try to present the matter in the most unobjectionable manner possible.

In reading over that marvelous account of creation I find frequent explicit declaration that God pronounced everything good after he had created it - except heaven and woman. I have maintained sometimes to stern, elderly ladies that this might have been an error of omission by early copyists, perpetuated and so become fixed in our translations. To other ladies, of other age and condition, to whom such propositions of scholarship might appear to be dull pedantry, I have ventured the gentlemanlike explanation that, as woman was the only living thing created that was good beyond doubt, perhaps God had paid her the special compliment of leaving the approval unspoken, as being in a sense supererogatory. At best, either of these dispositions of the matter is, of course, far-fetched, maybe even frivolous. The fact still remains by the record. And it is beyond doubt awkward and embarrassing, because ill-natured men can refer to it in moments of hatefulness - moments unfortunately too frequent.

Is it possible that this last creation was a mistake of Infinite Charity and Eternal Truth? That Charity forbore to acknowledge that it was a mistake and that Truth, in the very nature of its eternal essence, could not say it was good? It is so grave a matter that one wonders Helvetius did not betray it, as he did that other secret about which the philosophers had agreed to keep mum, so that Herr Schopenhauer could write about it as he did about that other. Herr Schopenhauer certainly had the courage to speak with philosophical asperity of the gentle sex. It may be because he was never married. And then his mother wrote novels! I have been surprised that he was not accused of prejudice.

But if all these everyday obstacles were absent there would yet remain insurmountable reasons why women can never be novel-readers in the sense that men are. Your wife, for instance, or the impenetrable mystery of womanhood that you contemplate making your wife some day - can you, honestly, now, as a self-respecting husband of either de facto or in futuro, quite agree to the spectacle of that adored lady sitting over across the hearth from you in the snug room, evening after evening, with her feet - however small and well-shaped - cocked up on the other end of the mantel and one of your own big colorado maduros between her teeth! We men, and particularly novel-readers, are liberal even generous, in our views; but it is not in human nature to stand that!

Now, if a woman can not put her feet up and smoke, how in the name of heaven, can she seriously read novels? Certainly not sitting bolt upright, in order to prevent the back of her new gown from rubbing the chair; certainly not reclining upon a couch or in a hammock. A boy, yet too young to smoke may properly lie on his stomach on the floor and read novels, but the mature veteran will fight for his end of the mantel as for his wife and children. It is physiological necessity, inasmuch as the blood that would naturally go to the lower extremities, is thus measurably lessened in quantity and goes instead to the head, where a state of gentle congestion ensues, exciting the brain cells, setting free the imagination to roam hand in hand with intelligence under the spell of the wizard. There may be novel-readers who do not smoke at the game, but surely they cannot be quite earnest or honest - you had better put in writing all business agreements with this sort.

*   *   *   *   *

No boy can ever hope to become a really great or celebrated novel-reader who does not begin his apprenticeship under the age of fourteen, and, as I said before, stick to it as long as he lives. He must learn to scorn those frivolous, vacillating and purposeless ones who, after beginning properly, turn aside and whiling away their time on mere history, or science, or philosophy. In a sense these departments of literature are useful enough. They enable you often to perceive the most cunning and profoundly interesting touches in fiction. Then I have no doubt that, merely as mental exercise, they do some good in keeping the mind in training for the serious work of novel-reading. I have always been grateful to Carlyle's "French Revolution," if for nothing more than that its criss-cross, confusing and impressive dullness enabled me to find more pleasure in "A Tale of Two Cities" than was to be extracted from any merit or interest in that unreal novel.

This much however, may be said of history, that it is looking up in these days as a result of studying the spirit of the novel. It was not many years ago that the ponderous gentlemen who write criticisms (chiefly because it has been forgotten how to stop that ancient waste of paper and ink) could find nothing more biting to say of Macaulay's "England" than that it was "a splendid work of imagination," of Froude's "Caesar" that it was "magnificent political fiction," and of Taine's "France" that "it was so fine it should have been history instead of fiction." And ever since then the world has read only these three writers upon these three epochs - and many other men have been writing history upon the same model. No good novel-reader need be ashamed to read them, in fact. They are so like the real thing we find in the greatest novels, instead of being the usual pompous official lies of old-time history, that there are flesh, blood and warmth in them.

In 1877, after the railway riots, legislative halls heard the French Revolution rehearsed from all points of view. In one capital, where I was reporting the debate, Old Oracle, with every fact at hand from "In the beginning" to the exact popular vote in 1876, talked two hours of accurate historical data from all the French histories, after which a young lawyer replied in fifteen minutes with a vivid picture of the popular conditions, the revolt and the result. Will it be allowable, in the interest of conveying exact impression, to say that Old Oracle was "swiped" off the earth? No other word will relieve my conscience. After it was all over I asked the young lawyer where he got his French history.

"From Dumas," he answered, "and from critical reviews of his novels. He's short on dates and documents, but he's long on the general facts."

Why not? Are not novels history?

Book for book, is not a novel by a competent conscientious novelist just as truthful a record of typical men, manners and motives as formal history is of official men, events and motives?

There are persons created out of the dreams of genius so real, so actual, so burnt into the heart and mind of the world that they have become historical. Do they not show you, in the old Ursuline Convent at New Orleans, the cell where poor Manon Lescaut sat alone in tears? And do they not show you her very grave on the banks of the lake? Have I not stood by the simple grave at Richmond, Virginia, where never lay the body of Pocahontas and listened to the story of her burial there? One of the loveliest women I ever knew admits that every time she visits relatives at Salem she goes out to look at the mound over the broken heart of

Hester Prynne, that dream daughter of genius who never actually lived or died, but who was and is and ever will be. Her grave can be easily pointed out, but where is that of Alexander, of Themistocles, of Aristotle, even of the first figure of history - Adam? Mark Twain found it for a joke. Dr. Hale was finally forced to write a preface to "The Man Without a Country" to declare that his hero was pure fiction and that the pathetic punishment so marvelously described was not only imaginary, but legally and actually impossible. It was because Philip Nolan had passed into history. I myself have met old men who knew sea captains that had met this melancholy prisoner at sea and looked upon him, had even spoken to him upon subjects not prohibited. And these old men did not hesitate to declare that Dr. Hale had lied in his denial and had repudiated the facts through cowardice or under compulsion from the War Department.

* * * * *

Indeed, so flexible, adaptable and penetrable is the style, and so admirably has the use and proper direction of the imagination been developed by the school of fiction, that every branch of literature has gained from it power, beauty and clearness. Nothing has aided more in the spread of liberal Christianity than the remarkable series of "Lives of Christ," from Straus to Farrar, not omitting particular mention of the singularly beautiful treatment of the subject by Renan. In all of these conscientious imagination has been used, as it is used in the highest works of fiction, to give to known facts the atmosphere and vividness of truth in order that the spirit and personality of the surroundings of the Savior of Mankind might be newly understood by and made fresh to modern perception.

Of all books it is to be said - of novels as well - that none is great that is not true, and that cannot be true which does not carry inherence of truth. Now every book is true to some reader. The "Arabian Nights" tales do not seem impossible to a little child, the only delight him. The novels of "The Duchess" seem true to a certain class of readers, if only because they treat of a society to which those readers are entirely unaccustomed. "Robinson Crusoe" is a gospel to the world, and yet it is the most palpably and innocently impossible of books. It is so plausible because the author has ingeniously or accidentally set aside the usual earmarks of plausibility. When an author plainly and easily knows what the reader does not know and enough more to continue the chain of seeming reality of truth a little further, he convinces the reader of his truth and ability. Those men, therefore, who have been endowed with the genius almost unconsciously to absorb, classify, combine, arrange and dispense vast knowledge in a bold, striking or noble manner, are the recognized greatest men of genius for the simple reason that the readers of the world who know most recognize all they know in these writers, together with that spirit of sublime imagination that suggests still greater realms of truth and beauty. What Shakesepare was to the intellectual leaders of his day, "The Duchess" was to countless immature young folks of her day who were looking for "something to read."

All truth is history, but all history is not truth. Written history is notoriously no well-cleaner.

III.

READING THE FIRST NOVEL
BEING MOSTLY REMINISCENCES OF EARLY
CRIMES AND JOYS

Once more and for all, the career of a novel reader should be entered upon, if at all, under the age of fourteen. As much earlier as possible. The life of the intellect, as of its shadowy twin, imagination, begins early and develops miraculously. The inbred strains of nature lie exposed to influence as a mirror to reflections, and as open to impression as sensitized paper, upon which pictures may be printed and from which they may also fade out. The greater the variety of impressions that fall upon the young mind the more certain it is that the greatest strength of natural tendency will be touched and revealed. Good or bad, whichever it may be, let it come out as quickly as possible. How many men have never developed their fatal weaknesses until success was within reach and the edifice fell upon other innocent ones. Believe me, no innate scoundrel or brute will be much helped or hindered by stories. These have no turn or leisure for dreaming. They are eager for the actual touch of life. What would a dull-eyed glutton, famishing, not with hunger but with the cravings of digestive ferocity, find in Thackeray's "Memorials of Gormandizing" or "Barmecidal Feasts?" Such banquets are spread for the frugal, not one of whom would swap that immortal cook-book review for a dinner with Lucullus. Rascals will not read. Men of action do not read. They look upon it as the gambler does upon the game where "no money passes." It may almost be said that the capacity for novel-reading is the patent of just and noble minds. You never heard of a great novel-reader who was notorious as a criminal. There have been literary criminals, I grant you - Eugene Aram Dr. Dodd, Prof. Webster, who murdered Parkmaan, and others. But they were writers, not readers And they did not write novels. Mr. Aram wrote scientific and school books, as did Prof. Webster, and Dr. Wainwright wrote beautiful sermons. We never do sufficiently consider the evil that lies behind writing sermons. The nearest you can come to a writer of fiction who has been steeped in crime is in Benvenuto Cellini, whose marvelous auto-biographical memoir certainly contains some fiction, though it is classed under the suspect department of History.

How many men actually have been saved from a criminal career by the miraculous influence of novels? Let who will deny, but at the age of six I myself was absolutely committed to the abandoned purpose of riding barebacked horses in a circus. Secretly, of course, because there were some vague speculations in the family concerning what seemed to be special adaptability to the work of preaching. Shortly after I gave that up to enlist in the Continental Army, under Gen. Francis Marion, and no other soldier slew more Britons. After discharge I at once volunteered in an Indiana regiment quartered in my native town in Kentucky, and beat the snare drum at the head of that fine body of men for a long time. But the tendency was downward. For three months I was chief of a of robbers that ravaged the backyards of the vicinity. Successively I became a spy for Washington, an Indian fighter, a tragic actor.

With character seared, abandoned and dissolute in habit through and by the hearing and seeing and reading of history, there was but one desperate step left So I entered upon the career of a pirate in my ninth year. The Spanish Main, as no doubt you remember, was at that time upon an open common across the street from our house, and it was a hundred feet long, half as wide and would average two feet in depth. I have often since thanked Heaven that they filled up that pathless ocean in order to build an iron foundry upon the spot. Suppose they had excavated for a cellar! Why during the time that Capt. Kidd, Lafitte and I infested the coast thereabout, sailing three "low, black-hulled schooners with long rakish masts," I forced hundreds of merchant seamen to walk the plank - even helpless women and children. Unless the sharks devoured them, their bones are yet about three feet under the floor of that iron foundry. Under the lee of the Northernmost promontory, near a rock marked with peculiar crosses made by the point of the stiletto which I constantly carried in my red silk sash, I buried tons of plate, and doubloons, pieces of eight, pistoles, Louis d'ors, and galleons by the chest. At that time galleons somehow meant to me money pieces in use, though since then the name has been given to a species of boat. The rich brocades, Damascus and Indian stuffs, laces, mantles, shawls and finery were piled in riotous profusion in our cave where - let the whole truth be told if it must - I lived with a bold, black-eyed and coquettish Spanish girl, who loved me with ungovernable jealousy that occasionally led to bitter and terrible scenes of rage and despair. At last when I brought home a white and red English girl whose life I spared because she had begged me her knees by the memory of my sainted mother to spare her for her old father, who was waiting her coming, Joquita passed all bounds. I killed her - with a single knife thrust I remember. She was buried right on the spot where the Tilden and Hendricks flag pole afterwards stood in the campaign of 1876. It was with bitter melancholy that I fancied the red stripes on the flag had their color from the blood of the poor, foolish jealous girl below.

*   *   *   *   *

Ah, well -

Let us all own up - we men of above forty who aspire to respectability and do actually live orderly lives and achieve even the odor of sanctity - have we not been stained with murder? - aye worse! What man has not his Bluebeard closet, full of early crimes and villainies? A certain boy in whom I take a particular interest, who goes to Sunday-school and whose life is outwardly proper - is he not now on week days a robber of great renown? A week ago, masked and armed, he held up his own father in a secluded corner of the library and relieved the old man of swag of a value beyond the dreams - not of avarice, but - of successful, respectable, modern speculation. He purposes to be a pirate whenever there is a convenient sheet of water near the house. God speed him. Better a pirate at six than at sixty.

Give them work to do and good novels to read and they will get over it. History breeds queer ideas in children. They read of military heroes, kings and statesmen who commit awful deeds and are yet monuments of public honor. What a sweet hero is Raleigh, who was a farmer of piracy; what a grand Admiral was Drake; what demi-gods the fighting Americans who murdered Indians for the crime of wanting their own! History hath charms to move an infant breast to savagery. Good strong novels are the best pabulum to nourish difference between virtue and vice.

Don't I know? I have felt the miracle and learned the difference so well that even now at an advanced age I can tell the difference and indulge in either. It was not a week after the killing of Joquita that I read the first novel of my life. It was "Scottish Chiefs." The dead bodies of ten thousand novels lie between me and that first one. I have not read it since. Ten Incas of Peru with ten rooms full of solid gold could not tempt me to read it again. Have I not a clear cinch on a delicious memory, compared with which gold is only Robinson Crusoe's "drug?" After a lapse of all these years the content of that one tremendous, noble chapter of heroic climax is as deeply burned into my memory as if it had been read yesterday.

A sister, old enough to receive "beaux" and addicted to the piano-forte accomplishment, was at that time practicing across the hall an instrumental composition, entitled, "La Rève." Under the title, printed in very small letters, was the English translation; but I never thought to look at it. An elocutionist had shortly before recited Poe's Raven at a church entertainment, and that gloomy bird flapped its wings in my young emotional vicinity when the firelight threw vague "shadows on the floor." When the piece of music was spoken as "La Rève," its sad cadences, suffering, of course, under practice, were instantly wedded in my mind to Mr.

Poe's wonderful bird and for years it meant the "Raven" to me. How curious are childish impressions. Years afterward when I saw a copy of the music and read the translation, "The Dream" under the title, I felt a distinct shock of resentment as if the French language had been treacherous to my sacred ideas. Then there was the romantic name of "Ellerslie," which, notwithstanding considerable precocity in reading and spelling I carried off as "Elleressie" Yeas afterward when the actual syllables confronted me in a historical sketch of Wallace, the truth entered like a stab and I closed the book. O sacred first illusions of childhood, you are sweeter than a thousand year of fame! It is God's providence that hardens us to endure the throwing of them down to our eyes and strengthens us to keep their memory sweet in our hearts.

* * * * *

It would be an affront then, not to assume that every reputable novel reader has read "Scottish Chiefs." If there is any descendant or any personal friend of that admirable lady, Miss Jane Porter, who may now be in pecuniary distress, let that descendant call upon me privately with perfect confidence. There are obligations that a glacial evolutionary period can not lessen. I make no conditions but the simple proof of proper identity. I am not rich but I am grateful.

It was a Saturday evening when I became aware, as by prescience, that there hung over Sir William Wallice and Helen Mar some terrible shadow of fate. And the piano-forte across the hall played "La Rève." My heart failed me and I closed the book. If you can't do that, my friend, then you waste your time trying to be a novel reader. You have not the true touch of genius for it. It is the miracle of eating your cake and having it, too. It must have been the unconscious moving of novel reading genius in me. For I forgot, as clearly as if it were not a possibility, that the next day was Sunday. And so hurried off, before time, to bed, to be alone with the burden on my heart.

"Backward, turn backward, O Time in your flight - Make me a child again just for tonight."

There are two or three novels I should love to take to bed as of yore - not to read, but to suffer over and to contemplate and to seek calmness and courage with which to face the inevitable. Could there be men base enough to do to death the noble Wallace? Or to break the heart of Helen Mar with grief? No argument could remove the presentiment, but facing the matter gave courage. "Let tomorrow answer," I thought, as the piano-forte in the next room played "La Rève." Then fell asleep.

And when I awoke next morning to the full knowledge that it was Sunday, I could have murdered the calendar. For Sunday was Dies Irae. After Sunday-school, at least. There is a certain amount of fun to be to extracted from Sunday-school. The remainder of those early Sundays was confined to reading the Bible or storybooks from the Sunday-school library - books, by the Lord Harry, that seem to be contrived especially to make out of healthy children life-long enemies of the church, and to bind hypocrites to the altar with hooks of steel. There was no whistling at all permitted; singing of hymns was encouraged; no "playing" - playing on Sunday was a distinct source of displeasure to Heaven! Are free-born men nine years of age to endure such tyranny with resignation? Ask the kids of today - and with one voice, as true men and free, they will answer you, "Nit!" In the dark days of my youth liberty was in chains, and so Sunday was passed in dreadful suspense as to what was doing in Scotland.

* * * * *

Monday night after supper I rejoined Sir William in his captivity and soon saw that my worst fears were to be realized. My father sat on the opposite side of the table reading politics; my mother was effecting the restoration of socks; my brother was engaged in unraveling mathematical tangles, and in the parlor across the hall my sister sat alone with her piano patiently debating "La Rève." Under these circumstances I encountered the first great miracle of intellectual emotion in the chapter describing the execution of William Wallace on Tower Hill. No other incident of life has left upon me such a profound impression. It was as if I had sprung at one bound into the arena of heroism. I remember it all. How Wallace delivered himself of theological and Christian precepts to Helen Mar after which they both knelt before the officiating priest. That she thought or said, "My life will expire with yours!" It was the keynote of death and life devotion. It was worthy to usher Wallace up the scaffold steps where he stood with his hands bound, "his noble head uncovered." There was much Christian edification, but the presence of such a hero as he with "noble Head uncovered" would enable any man nine years old with a spark of honor and sympathy in him to endure agonizing amounts of edification. Then suddenly there was a frightful shudder in my heart. The hangman approached with the rope, and Helen Mar, with a shriek, threw herself upon Wallace's breast. Then the great moment. If I live a thousand years these lines will always be with me: "Wallace, with a mighty strength, burst the bonds asunder that confined his arms and clasped her to his heart!"

* * * * *

In reading some critical or pretended text books on construction since that time I came across this sentence used to illustrate tautology. It was pointed out that the bonds couldn't be "burst" without necessarily being asunder. The confoundedest outrages in this world are the capers that precisionists cut upon the bodies of the noble dead. And with impunity too. Think of a village surveyor measuring the forest of Arden to discover the exact acreage! Or a horse-doctor elevating his eyebrow with a contemptuous smile and turning away, as from an innocent, when you speak of the wings of that fine horse, Pegasus! Any idiot knows that bonds couldn't be burst without being burst asunder. But, let the impregnable Jackass think - what would become of the noble rhythm and the majestic roll of sound? Shakespeare was an ignorant dunce also when he characterized the ingratitude that involves the principle of public honor as "the unkindest cut of all." Every school child knows that it is ungrammatical; but only those who have any sense learn after awhile the esoteric secret that it sometimes requires a tragedy of language to provide fitting sacrifice to the manes of despair. There never was yet a man of genius who wrote grammatically and under the scourge of rhetorical rules. Anthony Trollope is a most perfect example of the exact correctness that sterilizes in its own immaculate chastity. Thackeray would knock a qualifying adverb across the street, or thrust it under your nose to make room for the vivid force of an idea.

Trollope would give the idea a decent funeral for the sake of having his adverb appear at the grave above reproach from grammatical gossip. Whenever I have risen from the splendid psychological perspective of old Job, the solemn introspective howls of Ecclesiasticus and the generous living philosophy of Shakespeare it has always been with the desire - of course it is undignified, but it is human - to go and get an English grammar for the pleasure of spitting upon it. Let us be honest. I understand everything about grammar except what it means; but if you will give me the living substance and the proper spirit any gentleman who desires the grammatical rules may have them, and be hanged to him! And, while it may appear presumptuous, I can conscientiously say that it will not be agreeable to me to settle down in heaven with a class of persons who demand the rules of grammar for the intellectual reason that corresponds to the call for crutches by one-legged men.

* * * * *

If the foregoing appear ill-tempered pray forget it. Remember rather that I have sought to leave my friend Sir William Wallace, holding Helen Mar on his breast as long as possible. And yet, I also loved her! Can human nature go farther than that?

"Helen," he said to her, "life's cord is cut by God's own hand." He stooped, he fell, and the fall shook the scaffold. Helen - that glorified heroine - raised his head to her lap. The noble Earl of Gloucester stepped forward, took the head in his hands.

"There," he cried in a burst of grief, letting it fall again upon the insensible bosom of Helen, "there broke the noblest heart that ever beat in the breast of man!"

That page or two of description I read with difficulty and agony through blinding tears, and when Gloucester spoke his splendid eulogy my head fell on the table and I broke into such wild sobbing that the little family sprang up in astonishment. I could not explain until my mother, having led me to my room, succeeded in soothing me into calmness and I told her the cause of it. And she saw me to bed with sympathetic caresses and, after she left, it all broke out afresh and I cried myself to sleep in utter desolation and wretchedness. Of course the matter got out and my father began the book. He was sixty years old, not an indiscriminate reader, but a man of kind and boyish heart. I felt a sort of fascinated curiosity to watch him when he reached the chapter that had broken me. And, as if it were yesterday, I can see him under the lamplight compressing his lips, or puffing like a smoker through them, taking off his spectacles, and blowing his nose with great ceremony and carelessly allowing the handkerchief to reach his eyes. Then another paragraph and he would complain of the glasses and wipe them carefully, also his eyes, and replace the spectacles. But he never looked at me, and when he suddenly banged the lids together and, turning away, sat staring into the fire with his head bent forward, making unconcealed use of the handkerchief, I felt a sudden sympathy for him and sneaked out. He would have made a great novel reader if he had had the heart. But he couldn't stand sorrow and pain. The novel reader must have a heart for every fate. For a week or more I read that great chapter and its approaches over and over, weeping less and less, until I had worn out that first grief, and could look with dry eyes upon my dead. And never since have I dared to return to it. Let who will

speak freely in other tones of "Scottish Chiefs" -
opinions are sacred liberties - but as for me I know it
changed my career from one of ruthless piracy to better
purposes, and certain boys of my private acquaintance
are introduced to Miss Jane Porter as soon as they
show similar bent.

IV.

THE FIRST NOVEL TO READ CONTAINING SOME SCANDALOUS REMARKS ABOUT "ROBINSON CRUSOE"

The very best First-Novel-To-Read in all fiction is "Robinson Crusoe." There is no dogmatism in the declaration; it is the announcement of a fact as well ascertained as the accuracy of the multiplication table. It is one of the delights of novel reading that you may have any opinion you please and fire it off with confidence, without gainsay. Those who differ with you merely have another opinion, which is not sacred and cannot be proved any more than yours. All of the elements of supreme test of imaginative interest are in "Robinson Crusoe." Love is absent, but that is not a test; love appeals to persons who cannot read or write - it is universal, as hunger and thirst.

The book-reading boy is easily discovered; you always catch him reading books. But the novel-reading boy has a system of his own, a sort of instinctive way of getting the greatest excitement out of the story, the very best run for his money. This sort of boy soon learns to sit with his feet drawn up on the upper rung of a chair, so that from the knees to the thighs there is a gentle declivity of about thirty degrees; the knees are nicely separated that the book may lie on them without holding. That involves one of the most cunning of psychological secrets; because, if the boy is not a novel reader, he does not want the book to lie open, since every time it closes he gains just that much relief in finding the place again. The novel-reading boy knows the trick of immortal wisdom; he can go through the old book cases and pick the treasures of novels by the way they lie open; if he gets hold of a new or especially fine edition of his father's he need not be told to wrench it open in the middle and break the back of the binding - he does it instinctively.

There are other symptoms of the born novel reader to be observed in him. If he reads at night he is careful to so place his chair that the light will fall on the page from a direction that will ultimately ruin the eyes - but it does not interfere with the light. He humps himself over the open volume and begins to display that unerring curvalinearity of the spine that compels his mother to study braces and to fear that he will develop consumption. Yet you can study the world's health records and never find a line to prove that any man with "occupation or profession - novel reading" is recorded as dying of consumption. The humped-over attitude promotes compression of the lungs, tele-scoping of the diaphragm, atrophy of the abdominal abracadabra and other things (see Physiological Slush, p. 179, et seq.); but - it - never - hurts - the - boy!

To a novel reading boy the position is one of instinct, like that of the bicycle racer. His eyes are strained, his nerves and muscles at tension - everything ready for excitement - and the book, lying open, leaves his hands perfectly free to drum on the sides of the chair, slap his legs and knees, fumble in his pockets or even scratch his head as emotion or interest demand. Does anybody deny that the highest proof of special genius is the possession of the instinct to adapt itself to the matter in hand? Nothing more need be said.

* * * * *

Now, if you will observe carefully such a boy when he comes to a certain point in "Robinson Crusoe" you may recognize the stroke of fate in his destiny. If he's the right sort, he will read gayly along; he drums, he slaps himself, he beats his breast, he scratches his head. Suddenly there will come the shock. He is reading rapidly and gloriously. He finds his knife in his pocket, as usual, and puts it back; the top-string is there; he drums the devil's tattoo, he wets his finger and smears the margin of the page as he whirls it over and then - he finds - "The - Print - of - a - Man's - Naked - Foot - on - the - Shore!!!"

Oh, Crackey! At this tremendous moment the novel reader who has genius drums no more. His hands have seized the upper edges of the muslin lids, he presses the lower edges against his stomach, his back takes an added intensity of hump, his eyes bulge, his heart thumps - he is landed - landed!

Terror, surprise, sympathy, hope, skepticism, doubt - come all ye trooping emotions to threaten or console; but an end has come to fairy stories and wonder tales - Master Studious is in the awful presence of Human Nature.

* * * * *

For many years I have believed that that Print - of - a -

Man's - Naked - Foot was set in italic type in all editions of "Robinson Crusoe." But a patient search of many editions has convinced me that I must have been mistaken.

The passage comes sneaking along in the midst of a paragraph in common Roman letters and by the living jingo! you discover it just as Mr. Crusoe discovered the footprint itself!

No story ever written exhibits so profoundly either the perfect design of supreme genius or the curious accidental result of slovenly carelessness in a hack-writer. This is not said in any critical spirit, because, Robinson Crusoe, in one sense, is above criticism, and in another it permits the freest analysis without suffering in the estimation of any reader.

But for Robinson Crusoe, De Foe would never have ranked above the level of his time. It is customary for critics to speak in awe of the "Journal of the Plague" and it is gravely recited that that book deceived the great Dr. Meade. Dr. Meade must have been a poor doctor if De Foe's accuracy of description of the symptoms and effects of disease is not vastly superior to the detail he supplies as a sailor and solitaire upon a desert island. I have never been able to finish the "Journal." The only books in which his descriptions smack of reality are "Moll Flanders" and "Roxana," which will barely stand reading these days.

In what may be called its literary manner, Robinson Crusoe is entirely like the others. It convinces you by its own conviction of sincerity. It is simple, wandering yet direct; there is no making of "points" or moving to climaxes. De Foe did unquestionably possess the capacity to put into his story the appearance of sincerity that persuades belief at a glance. In that much he had the spark of genius; yet that same case has not availed to make the "Journal" of the Plague anything more than a curious and laborious conceit, while Robinson Crusoe stands among the first books of the world - a marvelous gleam of living interest, inextinguishably fresh and heartening to the imagination of every reader who has sensibility two removes above a toad.

The question arises, then, is "Robinson Crusoe" the calculated triumph of deliberate genius, or the accidental stroke of a hack who fell upon a golden suggestion in the account of Alexander Selkirk and increased its value ten thousand fold by an unintentional but rather perfect marshaling of incidents in order, and by a slovenly ignorance of character treatment that enhanced the interest to perfect intensity? This question may be discussed without undervaluing the book, the extraordinary merit of which is shown in the fact that, while its idea has been paraphrased, it has never been equalled. The "Swiss Family Robinson," the "Schonberg-Cotta Family" for children are full of merit and far better and more carefully written, but there are only the desert island and the ingenious shifts introduced. Charles Reade in "Hard Cash," Mr. Mallock in his "Nineteenth Century Romance," Clark Russel in "Marooned," and Mayne Reid, besides others, have used the same theater. But only in that one great book is the theater used to display the simple, yearning, natural, resolute, yet doubting, soul and heart of man in profound solitude, awaiting in armed terror, but not without purpose, the unknown and masked intentions of nature and savagery. It seems to me - and I have been tied to

Crusoe's chariot wheels for a dozen readings, I suppose - that it is the pressing in upon your emotions of the immensity of the great castaway's solitude, in which he appears like some tremendous Job of abandonment, fighting an unseen world, which is the innate note of its power.

* * * * *

The very moment Friday becomes a loyal subject, the suspense relaxes into pleased interest, and after Friday's funny father and the Spaniard and others appear it becomes a common book. As for the second part of the adventures I do not believe any matured man ever read it a second time unless for curious or literary purposes. If he did he must be one of that curious but simple family that have read the second part of "Faust," "Paradise Regained," and the "Odyssey," and who now peruse "Clarissa Harlowe" and go carefully over the catalogue of ships in the "Iliad" as a preparation for enjoying the excitements of the city directory.

Every particle of greatness in "Robinson Crusoe" is compressed within two hundred pages, the other four hundred being about as mediocre trash as you could purchase anywhere between cloth lids.

* * * * *

It is interesting to apply subjective analysis to Robinson Crusoe. The book in its very greatness has turned more critical swans into geese than almost any other. They have praised the marvelous ingenuity with which De Foe described how the castaway overcame single-handed, the deprivations of all civilized conveniences; they have marveled at the simple method in which all his labors are marshaled so as to render his conversion of the island into a home the type of industrial and even of social progress and theory; they have rhapsodized over the perfection of De Foe's style as a model of literary strength and artistic verisemblance. Only a short time ago a mighty critic of a great London paper said seriously that "Robinson Crusoe and Gulliver appeal infinitely more to the literary reader than to the boy, who does not want a classic but a book written by a contemporary." What an extraordinary boy that must be! It is probable that few boys care for Gulliver beyond his adventures in Lilliput and Brobdignag, but they devour that much, together with Robinson Crusoe, with just as much avidity now as they did a century ago. Your clear-headed, healthy boy is the first best critic of what constitutes the very liver and lights of a novel. Nothing but the primitive problems of courage meeting peril, virtue meeting vice, love, hatred, ambition for power and glory, will go down with him. The grown man is more capable of dealing with social subtleties and the problems of conscience, but those sorts of books do not last unless they have also "action - action - action."

Will the New Zealander, sitting amidst the prophetic ruins of St. Paul's, invite his soul reading Robert Elsmere? Of course you can't say what a New Zealander of that period might actually do; but what would you think of him if you caught him at it? The greatest stories of the world are the Bible stories, and I never saw a boy - intractable of acquiring the Sunday-school habit though he may have been - who wouldn't lay his savage head on his paws and quietly listen to the good old tales of wonder out of that book of treasures.

*   *   *   *   *

So let us look into the interior of our faithful old friend, Robinson Crusoe, and examine his composition as a literary whole. From the moment that Crusoe is washed ashore on the island until after the release of Friday's father and the Spaniard from the hands of the cannibals, there is no book in print, perhaps, that can surpass it in interest and the strained impression it makes upon the unsophisticated mind. It is all comprised in about 200 pages, but to a boy to whom the world is a theater of crowded action, to whom everything seems to have come ready-made, to whom the necessity of obedience and accommodation to others has been conveyed by constant friction - here he finds himself for the first time face to face with the problem of solitude. He can appreciate the danger from wild animals, genii, ghosts, battles, sieges and sudden death, but in no other book before, did he ever come upon a human being left solitary, with all these possible dangers to face.

The voyages on the raft, the house-building, contriving, fearing, praying, arguing - all these are full of plaintive pathos and yet of encouragement. He witnesses despair turned into comfortable resignation as the result of industry. It has required about twelve years. Virtue is apparently fattening upon its own reward, when - Smash! Bang! - our young reader runs upon "the - print - of - a - man's - naked - foot!" and security and happiness, like startled birds, are flown forever. For twelve more years this new unseen terror hangs over the poor solitary. Then we have Friday, the funny cannibals later and it is all over. But the vast solitude of that poor castaway has entered the imagination of the youth and dominates it.

These two hundred pages are crowded with suggestions that set a boy's mind on fire, yet every page contains evidence of obvious slovenliness, indolence and ignorance of human nature and common things, half of which faults seem directly to contribute to the result, while the other half are never noticed by the reader.

How many of you, who sniff at this, know Crusoe's real name? Yet it stares right out of the very first paragraphs in the book - a clean, perhaps accidental, proof of good scholarship, which De Foe possessed. Crusoe tells us his father was a German from Bremen, who married an Englishwoman, from whose family name of Robinson came the son's name which was properly Robinson Kreutznaer. This latter name, he explains, became corrupted in the common English speech into Crusoe. That is an excellent touch. The German pronunciation of Kreutznaer would sound like Krites-nare, and a mere dry scholar would have evolved Crysoe out of the name. But the English-speaking people everywhere, until within the past twenty years or so, have given the German "eu" the sound of "oo" or "u." Robinson's father therefore was called Crootsner until it was shaved into Crootsno and thence smoothed to Crusoe.

But what was the Christian name of the elder Kreutznaer? Or of the boy's mother? Or of his brothers or sisters? Or of the first ship captain under whom he sailed; or any of them; or even of the ship he commanded, and in which he was wrecked; or of the dog that he carried to the island; or of the two cats; or of the first and all the other tame goats; or of the inlet; or of Friday's father; or of the Spaniard he saved; or of the ship captain; or of the ship that finally saved him?

Young E. Allison

Who knows? The book is a desert as far as nomenclature goes - the only blossoms being his own name; that of Wells, a Brazilian neighbor; Xury, the Moorish boy; Friday, Poll, the parrot; and Will Atkins.

* * * * *

You may retort that all this doesn't matter. That is very true - and be hanged to you! - but those facts prove by every canon of literary art that Robinson Crusoe is either a coldly calculated flight of consummate genius or an accidental freak of hack literature. When De Foe wrote, it was only a century after Drake and his companions in authorized piracy had made the British privateer the scourge of the seas and had demonstrated that naval supremacy meant the control of the world. The seafaring life was one of peril, but it carried with it honor, glory and envy. Forty years later Nelson was born to crown British navalry with deathless Glory. Even the commonest sailor spoke his ship's name - if it were a fine vessel - with the same affection that he spoke his wife's and cursed a bad ship by its name as if to tag its vileness with proverbiality.

When De Foe wrote Alexander Selkirk, able seaman, was alive end had told his story of shipwreck to Sir Richard Steele, editor of the English Gentleman and of the Tattler, who wrote it up well - but not half as well as any one of ten thousand newspaper men of today could do under similar circumstances.

Now who that has read of Selkirk and Dampierre and Stradling does not remember the two famous ships, the "Cinque Ports" and the "St. George?" In every actvial book of the times, ship's names were sprinkled over the page as if they had been shaken out of the pepper box.

But you inquire in vain the name of the slaver that wrecked "poor Robinson Crusoe" - a name that would have been printed on his memory beyond forgetting because of the very misfortune itself. Now the book is the autobiography of a man whose only years of active life between eighteen and twenty-six were passed as a sailor. It was written apparently after he was seventy-two years old, at the period when every trifling incident and name of youth would survive most brightly; yet he names no ships, no sailor mates, carefully avoids all knowledge of or advantage attaching to any parts of ships. It is out of character as a sailor's tale, showing that the author either did not understand the value of or was too indolent to acquire the ship knowledge that would give to his work the natural smell of salt water and the bilge. It is a landlubber's sea yarn.

Is it in character as a revelation of human nature? No man like unto Robinson Crusoe ever did live, does live, or ever will live, unless as a freak deprived of human emotions. The Robinson Crusoe of Despair Island was not a castaway, but the mature politician. Daniel Defoe of Newgate Prison. The castaway would have melted into loving recollections; the imprisoned lampoonist would have busied himself with schemes, ideas, arguments and combinations for getting out, and getting on. This poor Robin on the island weeps over nothing but his own sorrows, and, while pretending to bewail his solitude, turns aside coldly from companionships next only in affection to those of men. He has a dog, two ship's cats (of whose "eminent history" he promises something that is never related), tame goats and parrots. He gives none of them a name, he does not occupy his yearning for companionship and love by preparing comforts for them or by teaching them tricks of intelligence or amusement; and when he does make a stagger at teaching Poll to talk it is for the sole purpose of hearing her repeat "Poor Robin Crusoe!" The dog is dragged in to work for him, but not to be rewarded. He dies without notice, as do the cats, and not even a billet of wood marks their graves.

Could any being, with a drop of human blood in his veins, do that? He thinks of his father with tears in his eyes - because he did not escape the present solitude by taking the old man's advice! Does he recall his mother or any of the childish things that lie so long and deep in the heart of every natural man? Does he ever wonder what his old school-fellows, Bob Freckles and Pete Baker, are doing these solitary evenings when he sits under the tropics and hopes - could he not at least hope it? - that they are, thank God, alive and happy at York? He discourses like a parson of the utterly impossible affection that Friday had for his cannibal sire and tells you how noble, Christian and beautiful it was - as if, by Jove! a little of that virtue wouldn't have ornamented his own cold, emotionless, fishy heart!

He had no sentimental side. Think of those dreary, egotistic, awful evenings, when, for more than twenty years this infernal hypocrite kept himself company and tried patiently to deceive God by flattering Him about religion! It is impossible. Why thought turns as certainly to revery and recollection as grass turns to seed. He married. What was his wife's name? We know how much property she had. What were the names of the honest Portuguese Captain and the London woman who kept his money? The cold selfishness and gloomy egotism of this creature mark him as a monster and not as a man.

*   *   *   *   *

So the book is not in character as an autobiography,
nor does it contain a single softening emotion to create
sympathy. Let us see whether it be scholarly in its
ease. The one line that strikes like a bolt of lightning is
the height of absurdity. We have all laughed, afterward
of course, at that - single - naked - foot - print. It could
not have been there without others, unless Friday were
a one legged man, or was playing the good old Scots
game of "hop-scotch!"

But the foot-print is not a circumstance to the
cannibals. All the stage burlesques of Robinson Crusoe
combined could not produce such funny cannibals as
he discovered. Crusoe's cannibals ate no flesh but that
of men! He had no great trouble contriving how to
induce Friday to eat goat's flesh! They took all the
trouble to come to his island to indulge in picnics,
during which they ate up folks, danced and then went
home before night. When the big party of 31 arrived,
they had with them one other cannibal of Friday's tribe,
a Spaniard, and Friday's father. It appears they always
carefully unbound a victim before despatching him.
They brought Friday pere for lunch, although he was
old, decrepit and thin - a condition that always unfits a
man among all known cannibals for serving as food.
They reject them as we do stringy old roosters for
spring chickens in the best society. Then Friday, born a
cannibal and converted to Crusoe's peculiar religion,
shows that in three years he has acquired all the
emotions of filial affection prevalent at that time
among Yorkshire folk who attended dissenting
chapels. More wonderful still! old Friday pere,
immersed in age and cannibalism, has the corresponding paternal feeling. Crusoe never says exactly

where these cannibals came from, but my own belief is that they came from that little Swiss town whence the little wooden animals for toy Noah's Arks also came.

A German savant - one of the patient sort that spend half a life writing a monograph on the variation of spots on the butterfly's wings - could get a philosophical dissertation on Doubt out of Crusoe's troubles with pens, ink and paper; also clothes. In the volume I am using, on page 86, third paragraph, he says: "I should lose my reckoning of time for want of books, and pen and ink." So he kept it by notches in wood, he tells in the fourth paragraph. In paragraph 5, same page, he says: "We are to observe that among the many things I brought out of the ship, I got several of less value, etc., which I omitted setting down as in particular pens, ink and paper!" Same paragraph, lower down: "I shall show that while my ink lasted I kept things very exact, but after that was gone I could not make any ink by any means that I could devise." Page 87, second paragraph: "I wanted many things, notwithstanding all the many things that I had amassed together, and of these ink was one!" Page 88, first paragraph: "I drew up my affairs in writing!" Now, by George! did you ever hear of more appearing and disappearing pens, ink and paper?

The adventures of his clothes were as remarkable as his own. On his very first trip to the wreck, after landing, he went "rummaging for clothes, of which I found enough," but took no more than he wanted for present use. On the second trip he "took all the men's clothes" (and there were fifteen souls on board when she sailed). Yet in his famous debit and credit calculations between good and evil he sets these down, page 88:

EVIL	GOOD
I have no clothes to cover me.	But I am in a hot climate, where, if I had clothes (!) I could hardly wear them.

On page 147, bewailing his lack of a sieve, he says: "Linen, I had none but what was mere rags."

Page 158 (one year later): "My clothes, too, began to decay; as to linen, I had had none a good while, except some checkered shirts, which I carefully preserved, because many times I could bear no other clothes on. I had almost three dozen of shirts, several thick watch coats, too hot to wear."

So he tried to make jackets out of the watch coats. Then this ingenious gentleman, who had nothing to wear and was glad of it on account of the heat, which kept him from wearing anything but a shirt, and rendered watch coats unendurable, actually made himself a coat, waistcoat, breeches, cap and umbrella of skins with the hair on and wore them in great comfort! Page 175 he goes hunting, wearing this suit, belted by two heavy skin belts, carrying hatchet, saw, powder, shot, his heavy fowling piece and the goatskin umbrella - total weight of baggage and clothes about ninety pounds. It must have been a cold day!

Yet the first thing he does for the naked Friday thirteen years later is to give him a pair - of - LINEN - trousers! Poor Robin Crusoe - what a colossal liar was wasted on a desert island!

* * * * *

Of course, no boy sees the blemishes in "Robinson Crusoe;" those are left to the Infallible Critic. The book is as ludicrous as "Hamlet" from one aspect and as profound as "Don Quixote" from another. In its pages the wonder tales and wonder facts meet and resolve; realism and idealism are joined - above all, there is a mystery no critic may solve. It is useless to criticize genius or a miracle, except to increase its wonder. Who remembers anything in "Crusoe" but the touch of the wizard's hand? Who associates the Duke of Athens, Hermia and Helena, with Bottom and Snug, Titania, Oberon and Puck? Any literary master mechanic might real off ten thousand yards of the Greek folks or of "Pericles," but when you want something that runs thus:

"I know a bank whereon the wild thyme blows!
Where oxlip and the nodding violet grows -."

why, then, my masters, you must put up the price and employ a genius to work the miracle.

Take all miracles without question. Whether work of genius or miracle of accident, "Robinson Crusoe" gives you a generous run for your money.

V

THE OPEN POLAR SEA OF NOVELS
WITH HIGHLY INCENDIARY ADVICE TO BOYS
AND SOME MORE ANCIENT HISTORY

After the first novel has been read, somewhere under the seasoned age of fourteen years, the beginner equipped with inherent genius for novel reading is afloat upon an open sea of literature, a master mariner of his own craft, having ports to make, to leave, to take, so splendid of variety and wonder as to make the voyages of Sinbad sing small by comparison. It may be proper and even a duty here to suggest to the young novel reader that the Ten Commandments and all governmental statutes authorize the instant killing, without pity or remorse, of any heavy-headed and intrusive person who presumes to map out for him a symmetrical and well-digested course of novel reading. The murder of such folks is universally excused as self-defense and secretly applauded as a public service. The born novel reader needs no guide, counsellor or friend. He is his own "master." He can with perfect safety and indescribable delight shut his eyes, reach out his hand, pull down any plum of a book and never make a mistake. Novel reading is the only one of the splendid occupations of life calling for no instruction or advice. All that is necessary is to bite the apple with the largest freedom possible to the intellectual and imaginative jaws, and let the taste of it squander itself all the way down from the front teeth until it is lost in the digestive joys of memory. There is no miserable quail limit to novels - you can read thirty novels in thirty days or 365 novels in 365 days for thirty years, and the last one will always have the delicious taste of the pies of childhood.

If any honest-minded boy chances to read these lines, let him charge his mind with full contempt for any misguided elders who have designs of "choosing only the best accepted novels" for his reading. There are no "best" novels except by the grace of the poor ones, and, if you don't read the poor ones, the "best" will be as tasteless as unsalted rice. I say to boys that are worth growing up: don't let anybody give you patronizing advice about novels. If your pastors and masters try oppression, there is the orchard, the creek bank, the attic room, the roof of the woodshed (under the peach tree), and a thousand other places where you may hide and maintain your natural independence. Don't let elderly and officious persons explain novels to you. They can not honestly do so; so don't waste time. Every boy of fourteen, with the genius to read 'em, is just as good a judge of novels and can understand them quite as well as any gentleman of brains of any old age. Because novels mean entirely different things to every blessed reader.

*   *   *   *   *

The main thing at the beginning is to be in the neighborhood of a good "novel orchard" and to nibble and eat, and even "gormandize," as your fancy leads you. Only - as you value your soul and your honor as a gentleman - bear in mind that what you read in every novel that pleases you is sacred truth. There are busy-bodies, pretenders to "culture," and sticklers for the multiplication table and Euclid's pestiferous theorem, who will tell you that novel reading is merely for entertainment and light accomplishment, and that the histories of fiction are purely imaginary and not to be taken seriously. That is pure falsehood. The truth of all humanity, as well as all its untruth, flows in a noble stream through the pages of fiction. Do not allow the elders to persuade you that pirate stories, battles, sieges, murders and sudden deaths, the road to transgression and the face of dishonesty are not good for you. They are 90 per cent. pure nutriment to a healthy boy's mind, and any other sort of boy ought particularly to read them and so learn the shortest cut to the penitentiary for the good of the world. Whenever you get hold of a novel that preaches and preaches and preaches, and can't give a poor ticket-of-leave man or the decentest sort of a villain credit for one good trait - Gee, Whizz! how tiresome they are - lose it, you young scamp, at once, if you respect yourself. If you are pushed you can say that Bill Jones took it away from you and threw it in the creek. The great Victor Hugo and the authors of that noble drama "The Two Orphans," are my authorities for the statement that some fibs - not all fibs, but some proper fibs - are entered in heaven on both debit and credit sides of the book of fate.

There is one book, the Book of Books, swelling rich and full with the wisdom and beauty and joy and sorrow of humanity - a book that set humility like a diamond in the forehead of virtue; that found mercy and charity outcasts among the minds of men and left them radiant queens in the world's heart; that stickled not to describe the gorgeous esotery of corroding passion and shamed it with the purity of Mary Magdelen; that dragged from the despair of old Job the uttermost poison-drop of doubt and answered it with the noble problem of organized existence; that teems with murder and mistake and glows with all goodness and honest aspiration - that is the Book of Books. There hasn't been one written since that has crossed the boundary of its scope. What would that book be after some goody-goody had expurgated it of evil and left it sterilized in butter and sugar? Let no ignorant paternal Czar, ruling over cottage or mansion, presume to keep from the mind and heart of youth the vigorous knowledge and observation of evil and good, crime and virtue together. No chaff, no wheat; no dross, no gold; no human faults and weaknesses, no heavenly hope. And if any gentleman does not like the sentiment, he can find me at my usual place of residence, unless he intends violence - and be hanged, also, to him!

*   *   *   *   *

A novel is a novel, and there are no bad ones in the world, except those you do not happen to like. Suppose a boy started with Robinson Crusoe and was scientifically and criminally steered by the hand of misguided "culture" to Scott and Dickens and Cooper and Hawthorne - all the classics, in fact, so that he would escape the vulgar thousands? Answer a straight question, ye old rooters between a thousand miles of muslin lids - would you have been willing to miss "The Gunmaker of Moscow" back yonder in the green days of say forty years ago? What do you think of Prof. William Henry Peck's "Cryptogram?" Were not Sylvanus Cobb, Jr., and Emerson Bennett authors of renown - honor to their dust, wherever it lies! Didn't you read Mrs. Southworth's "Capitola" or the "Hidden Hand" long before "Vashti" was dreamed of? Don't you remember that No. 52 of Beadle's Dime Library (light yellowish red paper covers) was "Silverheels, the Delaware," and that No. 77 was "Schinderhannes, the Outlaw of the Black Forest?" I yield to no man in affection and reverence for M. Dumas, Mr. Thackeray and others of the higher circles, but what's the matter with Ned Buntline, honest, breezy, vigorous, swinging old Ned? Put the "Three Guardsmen" where you will, but there is also room for "Buffalo Bill, the Scout." When I first saw Col. Cody, an ornament to the theatre and a painful trial to the drama, and realized that he was Buffalo Bill in the flesh - why, I was glad I had also read "Buffalo Bill's Last Shot" - (may he never shoot it). The day has passed forever, probably, when Buffalo Bill shall shout to his other scouts, "You set fire to the girl while I take care of the house!" or vice versa, and so saying, bear the fainting heroine triumphantly off from the treacherous redskins. But the story has lived.

* * * * *

It was a happy and honored custom in the old days for subscribers to the New York Ledger and the New York Weekly to unite in requests for the serial republication of favorite stories in those great fireside luminaries. They were the old-fashioned, broadside sheets and, of course, there were insuperable difficulties against preserving the numbers. After a year or two, therefore, there would awaken a general hunger among the loyal hosts to "read the story over," and when the demand was sufficiently strong the publishers would repeat it, cuts, divisions, and all, just as at first. How many times the "Gunmaker of Moscow" was repeated in the

Ledger, heaven knows. I remember I petitioned repeatedly for "Buffalo Bill" in the Weekly, and we got it, too, and waded through it again. By wading, I don't mean pushing laboriously and tediously through, but, by George! half immersion in the joy. It was a week between numbers, and a studious and appreciative boy made no bones of reading the current weekly chapters half a dozen times over while waiting for the next.

It must have been ten years later that I felt a thrill at the coming of Buffalo Bill himself in his first play. I had risen to the dignity of dramatic critic upon a journal of limited civilization and boundless politics, and was privileged to go behind the scenes at the theatre and actually speak to the actors. (I interviewed Mary Anderson during her first season, in the parlor of the local hotel, where honest George Bristow - who kept the cigar stand and could not keep a healthy appetite - always gave a Thanksgiving order for "two-whole-roast turkeys and a piece of breast," and they were served, too, the whole ones going to some near-by hospital, and the piece of breast to George's honest stomach - good, kind soul that he was. And Miss Anderson chewed gum during the whole period of the interview to the intense amusement of my elder and brother dramatic critic, who has since become the honored governor of his adopted state, and toward whom I beg to look with affectionate memory of those days.) Now, when a man has known novels intimately, has been dramatic critic, and has traveled with a circus, it seems to me in all reason he can not fairly have any other earthly joys to desire. At fifteen I was walking on tip-toe about the house on Sundays, and going off to the end of the garden to softly whistle "weekday" tunes, and at twenty I stood off the wings L. U. E., and had twenty "Black Crook" coryphees in silk tights and tarletan squeeze past in line, and nod and say, "Is it going all right in front?" They - knew - I - was - the - Critic! When you can do that you can laugh at Byron, roosting around upon inaccessible mountain crags and formulating solitude and indigestion into poetry!

I waited for Buffalo Bill's coming with feelings that can not be described. It was impossible to expect to meet Sir William Wallace in the flesh, or Sir Wilfred of Ivanhoe, or Capt. D'Artagnan, or Umslopogaas, or any one of a thousand great fighting heroes; but here was Buffalo Bill, just as great and glorious and dashing and handsome as any of them, and my right hand tingled to be grasped in that of the Bayard of the Prairies. And that hand's desire was attained. In his dressing-room between acts I sat nervously on a chair while the splendid Apollo of frontiersmen, in buckskin and beads, sat on his trunk, with his long, shapely legs sprawled gracefully out, his head thrown back so that the mane of brown hair should hang behind. It was glistening with oil and redolent of barber's perfume. And we talked there as one man to another, each apparently without fear. I was certainly nervous and timid, but he did not notice it, and I am frank to say he did not appear to feel the slightest personal fear of me. Thus, face to face, I saw the man with whom I had trod Ned Buntline's boundless plains and had seen and encountered a thousand perils and redskins. When the act call came, and I rose to go, a man stopped at the door and said to him:

"What shall it be to-night, Colonel?"

"A big beef-steak and a bottle of Bass!" answered Buffalo Bill heartily, "and tell 'ern to have it hot and ready at 11:15."

The beef-steak and Bass' ale were the watchwords of true heroism. The real hero requires substantial filling. He must have a head and a heart - but no less a good, healthy and impatient stomach.

In the daily paper the morning I write this I see the announcement of Buffalo Bill's "Wild West Show" coming two week's hence. Good luck to him! He can't charge prices too steep for me, and there are six seats necessary - the best in the amphitheater. And I wish I could be sure the vigorous spirit of Ned Buntline would be looking down from the blue sky overhead to see his hero charge the hill of San Juan at the head of the Rough Riders.

* * * * *

This digression may be wide of the subject of novel reading, but the real novel reader is at home anywhere. He has thoughts, dreams, reveries, fancies. All the world is his novel and all actions are stories and all the actors are characters. When Lucile Western, the excellent American actress, was at the height of her powers, not long before her last appearances, she had as her leading man a big, slouchy and careless person, who was advertised as "the talented young English actor, William Whally." In the intimacies of private association he was known as Bill Whally, and his descent was straight down from "Mount Sinai's awful height." He was a Hebrew and no better or more uneven and reckless actor ever played melodramatic "heavies." He had a love for Shakespeare, but could not play him; he had a love of drink and could gratify it. His vigorous talents purchased for him much forbearance. I've seen Mr. Whally play the fastidious and elegant "Sir Archibald Levison" in shiny black doe-skin trousers and old-fashioned cloth gaiters, because his condition rendered the problem of dressing somewhat doubtful, though it could not obscure his acting. He was the only walking embodiment of "Bill Sykes" I ever saw, and I contracted the habit of going to see him kill Miss Western as "Nancy" because he butchered that young woman with a broken chair more satisfactorily than anybody else I ever saw. There was a murderer for you - Bill Sykes! Bad as he was in most things, let us not forget that - he - killed - Nancy - and - killed - her - well and - thoroughly. If that young woman didn't snivel herself under a just sentence of death, I'm no fit householder to serve on a jury. Every time Miss Western came around it was my custom to read up fresh on "Oliver Twist" and hurry around and enjoy Bill Whally's happy application of retribution with the aid of the old property chair. There were six other persons whom I succeeded in persuading to applaud the scene with me every time it was acted.

But there's a separate chapter for villains.

* * * * *

Let us return to the old novels. What curious pranks time plays with tastes and vogues. Forty years ago N. P. Willis was just faded. Yet he was long a great comet of literary glitter and obscured many men of much greater ability. Everybody read him; the annuals hung upon his name; the ladies regarded him as a finer and more dashing Byron than Byron. The place he filled was much like that of Congreve, before whom Shakespeare's great nose was out of joint for a long time; Congreve, who was the margarita aluminata major of English poesy and drama and public life, and is now found in junk stores and in the back line on book shelves and whom nobody reads now. Willis had his languid affectations, his superficial cynicism and added to them ostentatious sentimentality.

Does anybody read William Gilmore Simm's elaborate rhetoric disguised as novels? He must have written two dozen of them, the Richardson of the United States. Lovers of delicious wit and intellectual humor still read Dr. Holmes' essays, but it would probably take a physician's prescription to make them swallow the novels. In what dark corners of the library are Bayard Taylor's novels and travels hidden? Will you come into the garden, Maud, and read Chancellor Walworth's mighty tragedies and Miss Mulock's Swiss-toy historical novels, or will you beg off, like the honest girl you are, and take a nap? Your sleepiness, dear Miss Maud, does you credit. By the way, what the deuce is the name of anyone of these novels? I can recall "Elsie Vernier," by Dr. Holmes and then there is a blank.

But what classics they were - then! In the thick of them had appeared a newspaper story that struggled through and was printed in book form. Old friends have told me how they waited at the country post-offices to get a copy, delayed for weeks. It was a scandal to read it in some localities. It was fiercely attacked as an outrageous exaggeration produced by temporary excitement and hostile feeling, or praised as a new gospel. It has been translated into every tongue having a printing press, and has sold by millions of copies. It was "Uncle Tom's Cabin." It was not a classic, but what a vigorous immortal mongrel of human sentiment it was! What a row was kicked up over Miss Braddon's "Octoroon," and what an impossible yellowback it was! The toughest piece of fiction I met with as a boy was "Sanford and Merton," and I've been aching to say so for four pages. If this world were full of Sanfords and Mertons, then give me Jupiter or some other comfortable planet at a secure sanitary distance removed.

I can't even remember the writers who were grammatically and rhetorically perfect forty years ago, and also very dull with it all. Is there a bookshelf that holds "Leni Leoti, or The Flower of the Prairies?" There are "Jane Eyre," "Lady Audley's Secret," and "John Halifax, Gentleman," which will go with many and are all well worth the reading, too. Are Mrs. Eliza A. Dupuy, Mrs. E. D. E. N. Southworth, Mrs. Caroline Lee Hentz and Augusta J. Evans dead? Their novels still live - look at the book stores. "Linda, or the Young Pilot of the Belle Creole," "India, the Pearl of Pearl River," "The Planter's Northern Bride," "St. Elmo" - they were fiction for you! A boy old enough to have a first sweetheart could swallow them by the mile.

You remember, when we were boys, the circus acrobats always - always, remember - rubbed young children with snake-oil and walloped them with a rawhide to educate them in tumbling and contortion? Well, if I could get the snake-oil for the joints and a curly young wig, I'd like to get back at five hundred of those books and devour them again - "as of yore!"

VI

RASCALS
BEING A DISCOURSE UPON GOOD, HONEST SCOUNDRELISM AND VILLAINS.

The people that inhabit novels are like other peoples of the earth - if they are peaceful, they have no history. So that, therefore, in novels, as in nations, it is the great restless heights of society that are to be approached with greatest awe and that engage admiration and regard. Everybody is interested in Nero, but not one person in ten thousand can tell you anything definite about Constantine or even Marcus Aurelius. If you should speak off-handedly about Amelia Sedley in the presence of a thousand average readers you would probably miss 85 per cent. of effect; if you said Becky Sharp the whole thousand would understand.

There is this to be said of disreputable folk, that they are clever and picturesque and interesting, at least.

An elderly jeweler in New York City was arrested several years ago upon the charge of receiving stolen gold and silver plate, watches and jewelry from well-known thieves. For forty years he had been a respected merchant, a church officer, a husband, father, and citizen, of irreproachable reputation, with enduring friendships. He was charitable, liberal and kindly. For decade after decade he was the experienced, wise and fatherly "fence" of professional burglars and thieves. Why, it would be an education in itself to know that man, to shake his honest hand, fresh from charity or concealment, and smoke a pipe with him and hear him talk about things frankly. When he gave to the missionary collection, rest assured he gave sincerely; when he "covered swag," into the melting pot for an industrious burglar, he did so only in the regular course of business.

Strange as it may seem, even criminals have human feelings in common with all of us. The old Thug who stepped aside into the bushes and prayed earnestly while his son was throwing his first strangling cloth around the throat of the English traveler - prayed for that son's honorable, successful beginning in his life devotion - was a good father. And when he was told that the son had acted with unusual skill, who can doubt that his tears of joy were sincere and humble tears of thankfulness? At least Bowanee knew. Can you not imagine a kind-hearted Chinese matron saying to her neighbor over the bamboo fence, "Yes, we sent the baby down to the beach (or the river bank or the forest) yesterday. We couldn't afford to keep it. I hope the gods have taken its little soul. At any rate it is sure of salvation hereafter."

*   *   *   *   *

Some twenty years ago I took the night train from Pineville to Barbourville, in the Kentucky mountains, reaching the latter place about 11 o'clock of a cold, rainy, dark November night. Only one other passenger alighted. There was an express wagon to take us to the town, a mile or so distant, and the wagon was already heavy with freight packages. The road was through a narrow lane, hub-deep with mud, and what, with stalling and resting, we were more than half an hour getting to the hotel. My fellow passenger was about my age, and was a shrewd, well-informed native of the vicinity. He knew the mineral, timber and agricultural resources, was evidently an enterprising business man and an intelligent but not voluble talker. He accepted a cigar, and advised me to see the house in Barbourville where the late Justice Samuel Miller was born. At the hotel he registered first, and, as he was going to leave next day and I was to remain several days, he told the clerk to give me the better of the two rooms vacant. It was a very pleasant act of thoughtfulness. The name on the register was "A. Johnson." The next day I asked the clerk about Mr. Johnson. My fellow passenger was Andy Johnson, whose fame as a feud-fighter and slayer of men has never been exceeded in the history of mountain feuds. He then had three or four men to his credit, definitely, and several doubtful ascriptions. He added a few more, I believe, before he met the inevitable.

Now, while Mr. Johnson, in all matters where killing seemed to him to be appropriate, was a most prompt and accurate man in accomplishing it, yet he was not the murderer that ignorant and isolated folks conceive such persons to be. The cigar I had given him was a very bad, cheap cigar, and, if he had merely wanted murder, he had every reason to kill me for giving it to him, and he had a perfect night for the deed. But he smoked it to the stub without a complaint or remark and saw that I got the best room in the hotel. Johnson was a cautious and considerate fellow-man, whose murders were doubtless private hobbies and exercises growing out of his environment and heredity.

One of the houses I most delight to enter in a certain town is one where I am always sure to see a devoted and happy wife and beautiful, playful children clustering around the armchair in which sits a man who committed one of the most cold-blooded assassinations you can imagine. He is an honored, esteemed and model citizen. His acquittal was a miracle in a million chances. He has justified it. It is beautiful to see those happy children clinging to the hand that -

Well, dear friends, the dentist is not a cruel man in his social capacity, and you can get delicious viands instead of nauseous medicines at the doctor's private table.

That is why beginning novel readers should take no advice. Strike out alone through the highways and lanes of story, character and experience. The best novelist is the one who fears not to tell you the truth, which is more wonderful than fiction. It is always the best hearts that bend to mistakes. Absolute virtue is as sterile as granite rock; absolute vice is as poisonous as a stagnant pond. No healthy interest or speculation can linger about either. Enter into the struggle and know human nature; don't stay outside and try to appear superior.

For, which of us has not his crimes of thought to account for? Think not, because Andy Johnson or William Sykes or Dr. Webster actually killed his man, that you are guiltless, because you haven't. Have you never wanted to? Answer that, in your conscience and in solitude - not to me. Speak up to yourself and then say whether the difference between you and the recorded criminal is not merely the difference between the overt act and the faltering wish. It is a matter of courage or of custom. Speaking for one gentleman, who knows himself and is not afraid to confess, I can say that, while he could not kill a mouse with his own hand, he has often murdered men in his heart. It may have been in fiery youth over the wrong name on a dancing card, or, later, when a rival got the better of him in discussion, or, when the dreary bore came and wouldn't go, or, when misdirected goodness insisted on thrusting upon him intended kindness that was wormwood and poison to the soul. Are we not covetous (not confessedly, of course, but actually)? Is not covetousness the thwarted desire of theft without courage? How many of us, now - speaking man to man - can open up our veiled thoughts and desires and then look the Ten Commandments in the eye without blushing?

*   *   *   *   *

The bravest, noblest, gentlest gentleman I have ever known was the Count de la Fere, whom we at the Hotel de Troisville, in old Paris, called "Athos." He was not merely sans peur et sans reproche as Bayard, but was positive in his virtues. He fought for his friends without even asking the cause of the fray. Yet, what a prig he seemed to be at first, with his eternal gentle melancholy, his irreproachable courtesy, unvarying kindness and complete unselfishness. You cannot - quite - warm - to - a - man - who - is - so - perfectly - right - that - he - embarrasses - everybody - but - the - angels.

But, when he ordered the gloomy and awful death of the treacherous Miladi, woman though she was, and thus as a perfect gentleman took on human frailty also, ah! how attractively noble and strong he became I In that respect he was the antithetical corollary of William Sykes, who was a purposeless, useless and uninterestingly regular scoundrel, thief and brute, until he redeemed himself by becoming the instrument of social justice and pounding that unendurable lady, Miss Nancy, of his name, into absence from the world. Perhaps I have remarked before - and even if I have it is pleasant to repeat it - that Bill Sykes had his faults, as also have most of us, but it was given to him to earn forgiveness by the aid of a cheap chair and the providential propinquity of Miss Nancy. I never think of it without regretting that poor Bill Whally is dead. He did it - so - much - to - my - taste!

Who shall we say is the most loved and respected criminal in fiction? Not Monsignor Rodin, of "The Wandering Jew;" not Thenardier in "Les Miserables." These are really not criminals; they are allegorical figures of perfect crime. They are solar centers, so far off and fixed that one may regard them only with awe, reverence and fear. They are types of fate, desire, temptation and chastisement. Let us turn to our own flesh and blood and speak gratefully of them.

*   *   *   *   *

Who says Count Fosco? Now there is a criminal worthy of affection and confidence. What an expansive nature, with kindness presented on every side. Even the dogs fawned upon him and the birds came at his call. An accomplished gentleman, considerately mannered - queer, as becomes a foreigner, yet possessing the touchstone of universal sympathy. Another man with crime to commit almost certainly would have dispatched it with ruthless coldness; but how kindly and gently Count Fosco administered the cord of necessity. With what delicacy he concealed the bowstring and spoke of the Bosphorus only as a place for moonlight excursions. He could have presented prussic acid and sherry to a lady in such a manner as to render the results a grateful sacrifice to his courtesy. It was all due to his corpulence; a "lean and hungry" villain lacks repose, patience and the tact of good humor. In almost every small social and individual attitude Count Fosco was human. He was exceedingly attentive to his wife in society and bullied her only in private and when necessary. He struck no dramatic attitudes. "The world is mine oyster!" is not said by real men bent on terrible deeds. Count Fosco is the perfect villain, and also the perfect criminal, inasmuch as he not only acts naturally, but deliberately determines the action instead of being drawn into it or having it forced upon him.

He was a highly cultivated type of Andy Johnson, inasmuch as crime with him was not a life purpose, but what is called in business a "side-line." All of us have our hobbies; the closely confined clerk goes home and roots up his yard to plant flower bulbs or cabbage plants; another fancies fowls; another man collects pewter pots and old brass and the millionaire takes to priceless horses; others of us turn from useful statistics and go broke on novels or poetry or music. Count Fosco was an educated gentleman and the pleasure of life was his purpose; crime and intrigue were his recreations. Andy Johnson was a good business man and wealth producer; murder was the direction in which his private understanding of personal disagreements was exercised and vented. Some men turn to poker playing, which is as wasteful as murder and not half as dignified. Count Fosco is the villain par excellence of novels. I do not remember what he did, because "The Woman in White" is the best novel in the world to read gluttonously at a sitting and then forget absolutely. It is nearly always a new book if you use it that way. When the world is dark, the fates bilious, the appetite dead and the infernal twinges of pain or sickness seem beyond reach of the doctor, "The Woman in White" is a friend indeed.

*   *   *   *   *

But the man of men for villains, not necessarily criminals; but the ordinary, every-day, picturesque worthies of good, honest scoundrelism and disreputableness is Sir Robert Louis Stevenson. You can afford conscientiously to stuff ballot boxes in order that his election may be secured as Poet Laureate of Rascals. Leaving out John Silver and Billy Bones and Alan Breck, whom every privately shriven rascal of us simply must honor and revere as giants of courage, cunning and controlled, conscience, Stevenson turned from singles and pairs, and in "The Ebb Tide," drove, by turns, tandem and abreast, a four-in-hand of scoundrels so buoyant, natural, strong, and yet each so totally unlike the others, that every honest novel reader may well be excused for shedding tears when he reflects that the marvelous hand and heart that created them are gone forever from the haunts of the interestingly wicked. No novelist ever exposed the human nature of rascals as Stevenson did.

Now, Iago was not a villain; he was a venomous toad, a scorpion, a mad-dog, a poisonous plant in a fair meadow. There was nobody Iago loved, no weakness he concealed, no point of contact with any human being. His sister was Pandora, his brother made the shirt of Nessus, himself dealt in Black Plagues and the

Leprosy. The old Serpent was permitted to rise from his belly and walk upright on the tip of his tail when he met Iago, as a demonstration of moral superiority. But think of those three Babes-in-the-Wood villains, skipper Davis, the Yankee swashbuckler and ship scuttler; Herrick, the dreamy poet, ruined by commerce and early love, with his days of remorse and his days of compensatary liquor; and Huish, the great-hearted Scotch ruffian, who chafed at the conventional concealments of trade among pals and never could - as a true Scotchman - understand why you should wait to use a knife upon a victim when promptness lay in the club right at hand - think of them sailing out of Honolulu harbor on the Farallone.

Let who will prefer to have sailed with Jason or Aeneas or Sinbad; but the Farallone and its precious freight of rascality gets my money every time. Think of the three incomparable reprobates afloat, with one case of smallpox and a cargo of champagne, daring to make no port, with over a hundred million square miles of ocean around them, every ten lookout knots of it containing a possible peril! It was simply grand - not pirates, shipwrecks or mutinies could beat that problem. And the pathos of the sixth day, when, with every man Jack of them looking delirium tremens in the face and suspecting each the other, Mr. Huish opened a new case of champagne and - found clear spring water under the French label! The honest scoundrels had been laid by the heels by a common wine merchant in the regular way of business! Oh, gentlemen, there should be honor in business; so that gallant villains can be free of betrayal.

The keynote of these gentlemen is struck in the second chapter, where all three of them writing lies home -

Davis and Herrick, sentimental equivocations, Huish the strongest of brag with nobody to send it to. In a burst of weakness Davis tells Herrick what a villain he has been, through rum, and how he can not let his daughter, "little Adar," know it. "Yes, there was a woman on board," he said, describing the ship he had scuttled. "Guess I sent her to hell, if there's such a place. I never dared go home again, and I don't know," he added, bitterly, "what's come to them."

"Thank you, Captain," said Herrick, "I never liked you better!"

Is it not in human nature to cuddle to a great sheepish murderer like that, who groans in secret for his little girl - if even the girl was truth? I think she turned out a myth, but he had the sentiment.

Was there ever a more melancholy, remorse-stricken wretch than Cap'n Davis? Or a gentler and seedier poet than Herrick? Or a more finely sodden and soaked old rum sport than Huish (not - Whish!) But it was not until they fell in with Attwater that their weakness as scoundrels was exposed. Attwater was so splendidly religious! He was determined to have things right if he had to have them so by bloodshed; he saved souls by bullets. Things were right when they were as he thought they should be. And believing so, with Torquemada, Alexander Sixtus and other most religious brethren, he was ready to set up the stake and fagot and cauterize sin with fire. One thing you can say about the religious folks that are big with cocksureness and a mission - they may make mistakes, but the mistake doesn't talk and criticise.

*   *   *   *   *

The only rascal worthy to travel in company with Stevenson's rascals is the Chevalier Balibari, of Castle Barry, in Ireland, whose admirable memoirs have been so well told by Mr. Thackeray. The Baron de la Motte in "Denis Duval," was advantageously born to ornament the purple and fine linen of picturesque unrighteousness - but his was a brief star that fell unfinished from its place amidst the Pleiades. Thackeray's genius ran more to disreputable men than to actual villains. But he drew two scoundrels that will serve as beacon lights to any clean-souled youth with the instinct to take warning. One was Lord Steyne, the other, Dr. George Brand Firmin; one the aristocratic, class-bred, cynical brute, the other the cold, tuft-hunting trained hypocrite. What encouragement of self-respect Judas Iscariot might have received if he had met Dr. Firmin!

Dr. Chadband, Mr. Pecksniff, Bill Sykes, Fagin, Mr. Murdstone, of Dickens' family - they are all strong in impression, but wholly unreal; mere stage villains and caricatures. A villain who has no good traits, no hobbies of kindness and affection, is never born into the world; he is always created by grotesque novel writers.

The villains of Dumas, Hugo, Balzac, Daudet are French. There may have been, or may be now such prototypes alive in France - because the Dreyfus case occurred in France, and no doubt much can happen in that fine, fertile country which translators cannot fully convey over the frontiers; but they have always seemed to me first cousins to my friends, the ogres, the evil magicians and the werewolves, and, in that much, not quite natural.

For heroes of the genuine cavalleria type, plumed, doubleted, pumpt and magnificent, give me Dumas; for good folks and true, the great American Fenimore Cooper; but for the blessed company of blooming, breathing rascals, Stevenson and Thackeray all the time.

VII

HEROES
THE NATURE AND THE FLOWER OF THEM -
THE GALLANT D'ARTAGNAN OR THE
GLORIOUS BUSSY.

Let us agree at the start that no perfect hero can be entirely mortal. The nearer the element of mortality in him corresponds to the heel measure of Achilles, the better his chance as hero. The Egyptian and Greek heroes were invariably demi-gods on the paternal or maternal side. Few actual historic heroes have escaped popular scandal concerning their origin, because the savage logic in us demands lions from a lion; that Theseus shall trace to Mars; that courage shall spring from courage.

Another most excellent thing about the ideal hero is that the immortal quality enables him to go about the business of his heroism without bothering his head with the rights or wrongs of it, except as the prevailing sentiment of social honor (as distinguished from the inborn sentiment of honesty) requires at the time. Of course, there is a lower grade of measly, "moral heroes," who (thank heaven and the innate sense of human justice!) are usually well peppered with sorrow and punishment. The hero of romance is a different stripe; Hyperion to a Satyr. He doesn't go around groaning page after page of top-heavy debates as to the inherent justice of his cause or his moral right to thrust a tallow candle between the particular ribs behind which the heart of his enemy is to be found - balancing his pros and cons, seeking a quo for each quid, and conscientiously prowling for final authorities. When you invade the chiropodical secret of the real hero's fine boot, or brush him in passing - if you have looked once too often at a certain lady, or have stood between him and the sun, or even twiddled your thumbs at him in an indecorous or careless manner - look to it that you be prepared to draw and mayhap to be spitted upon his sword's point, with honor. Sdeath! A gentlemen of courage carries his life lightly at the needle end of his rapier, as that wonderful Japanese, Samsori, used to make the flimsiest feather preside in miraculous equilibration upon the tip of his handsome nose.

No hero who does more or less than is demanded by the best practical opinion of the society of his time is worth more than thirty cents as a hero. Boys are literary and dramatic critics so far above the critics formed by strained formulas of the schools that you can trust them. They have an unerring distrust of the fellow who moves around with his confounded conscientious scruples, as if the well-settled opinion of the breathing world were not good enough for him! Who the deuce has got any business setting everybody else right?

Some of these days I believe it is going to be discovered that the atmosphere and the encompassing radiance and sweetness of Heaven are composed of the dear sighs and loving aspirations of earthly mother-hood. If it turns out otherwise, rest assured Heaven will not have reached its perfect point of evolution. Why is it, then, that mothers will - will - will - try, so mistakenly, to extirpate the jewel of honest, manly savagery from the breasts of their boys? I wonder if they know that when grown men see one of these "pretty-mannered boys," cocksure as a Swiss toy new painted and directed by watch spring, they feel an unholy impulse to empty an ink-bottle over the young calf? Fauntleroy kids are a reproach to our civilization. Men, women and children, all of us, crowd around the grimy Deignan of the Merrimac crew, and shout and cheer for Bill Smith, the Rough Rider, who carried his mate out of the ruck at San Juan and twirls his hat awkwardly and explains: "Ef I hadn't a saw him fall he would 'a' laid thar yit!" - and go straight home and pretend to be proud of a snug little poodle of a man who doesn't play for fear of soiling his picture-clothes, and who says: "Yes, sir, thank you," and "No, thank you, ma'am," like a French doll before it has had the sawdust kicked out of it!

* * * * *

Now, when a hero tries to stamp his acts with the precise quality of exact justice - why, he performs no acts. He is no better than that poor tongue-loose Hamlet, who argues you the right of everything, and then, by the great Jingo! piles in and messes it all by doing the wrong thing at the wrong time and in the wrong manner. It is permitted of course to be a great moral light and correct the errors of all the dust of earth that has been blown into life these ages; but human justice has been measured out unerringly with poetry and irony to such folk. They are admitted to be saints, but about the time they have got too good for their earthly setting, they have been tied to stakes and lighted up with oil and faggots; or a soda phosphate with a pinch of cyanide of potassium inserted has been handed to them, as in the case of our old friend, Socrates. And it's right. When a man gets too wise and good for his fellows and is embarrassed by the healthful scent of good human nature, send him to heaven for relief, where he can have the goodly fellowship of the prophets, the company of the noble army of martyrs, and amuse himself suggesting improvements upon the vocal selections of cherubim and seraphim! Impress the idea upon these gentry with warmth - and - with - oil!

*   *   *   *   *

The ideal hero of fiction, you say, is Capt. D'Artagnan, first name unknown, one time cadet in the Reserves of M. de Troisville's company of the King's Guards, intrusted with the care of the honor and safety of His Majesty, Louis XIV. Very well; he is a noble gentleman; the choice does honor to your heart, mind and soul; take him and hold the remembrance of his courage, loyalty, adroitness and splendid endurance with hooks of steel. For myself, while yielding to none who honor the great D'Artagnan, yet I march under the flag of the Sieur Bussy d'Amboise, a proud Clermont, of blood royal in the reign of Henry III., who shed luster upon a court that was edified by the wisdom of M. Chicot, the "King's Brother," the incomparable jester and philosopher, who would have himself exceeded all heroes except that he despised the actors and the audience of the world's theater and performed valiant feats only that he might hang his cap and bells upon the achievements in ridicule.

Can it be improper to compare D'Artagnan and Bussy -

when the intention is wholly respectful and the motive pure? If a single protest is heard, there will be an end to this paper now - at once. There are some comparisons that strengthen both candidates. For, we must consider the extent of the theater and the stage, the space of time covering the achievements, the varying conditions, lights and complexities. As, for instance, the very atmosphere in which these two heroes moved, the accompaniment of manner which we call the "air" of the histories, and which are markedly different. The contrast of breeding, quality and refinement between Bussy and D'Artagnan is as great as that which distinguishes Mercutio from the keen M. Chicot. Yet each was his own ideal type. Birth and the superior privileges of the haute noblesse conferred upon the Sieur Bussy the splendid air of its own sufficient prestige; the lack of these require of D'Artagnan that his intelligence, courage and loyal devotion should yet seem to yield something of their greatness in the submission that the man was compelled to pay to the master. True, this attitude was atoned for on occasion by blunt boldness, but the abased position and the lack of subtle distinction of air and mind of the noble, forbade to the Fourth Mousquetaire the last gracious touch of a Bayard of heroism. But the vulgarity was itself heroic.

* * * * *

Compare the first appearance of the great Gascon at the Hotel de Troisville, or even his manner and attitude toward the King when he sought to warn that monarch against forgetfulness of loyalty proved, with the haughty insolence of indomitable spirit in which Bussy threw back to Henry the shuttle of disfavor on the night of that remarkable wedding of St. Luc with the piquant little page soubrette, Jeanne de Brissac.

D'Artagnan's air to his King has its pathos. It seems to say: "I speak bluntly, sire, knowing that my life is yours and yet feeling that it is too obscure to provoke your vengeance." A very hard draught for a man of fire and fearlessness to take without a gulp. But into Bussy's manner toward his King there was this flash of lightning from Olympus: "My life, sire, is yours, as my King, to take or leave; but not even you may dare to think of taking the life of Bussy with the dust of least reproach upon it. My life you may blow out; my honor you do not dare approach to question!"

There are advantages in being a gentleman, which can not be denied. One is that it commands credit in the King's presence as well as at the tailor's.

It is interesting to compare both these attitudes with that of "Athos," the Count de la Fere, toward the King. He was lacking in the irresistibly fierce insolence of Bussy and in the abasement of D'Artagnan; it was melancholy, patient, persistent and terrible in its restrained calmness. How narrowly he just escaped true greatness. I would no more cast reproaches upon that noble gentleman than I would upon my grand-mother; but he - was - a - trifle - serous, wasn't he? He was brave, prompt, resourceful, splendid, and, at need, gingerish as the best colt in the paddock. It is the deuce's own pity for a man to be born to too much seriousness. Do you know - and as I love my country, I mean it in honest respect - that I sometimes think that the gentleness and melancholy of Athos somehow suggests a bit of distrust. One is almost terrified at times lest he may begin the Hamlet controversies. You feel that if he committed a murder by mistake you are not absolutely sure he wouldn't take a turn with Remorse. Not so Bussy; he would throw the mistake in with good will and not create worry about it. Hang it all, if the necessary business of murder is to halt upon the shuffling accident of mistake, we may as well sell out the hero business and rent the shop. It would be down to the level of Hamlet in no time. Unless, of course, the hero took the view of it that Nero adopted. It is improbable that Nero inherited the gift of natural remorse; but he cultivated one and seemed to do well with it. He used to reflect upon his mother and his wife, both of whom he had affectionately murdered, and justified himself by declaring that a great artist, who was also the Roman Emperor, would be lacking in breadth of emotional experience and retrospective wisdom, unless he knew the melancholy of a two-pronged family remorse. And from Nero's standpoint it was one of the best thoughts that he ever formulated into language.

To return to Bussy and D'Artagnan. In courage they were Hector and Achilles. You remember the champagne picnic before the bastion St. Gervais at the siege of St. Rochelle? What light-hearted gayety amid the flying missiles of the arquebusiers! Yet, do not forget that - ignoring the lacquey - there were four of them, and that his Eminence, the Cardinal Duke, had said the four of them were equal to a thousand men! If you have enough knowledge of human nature to understand the fine game of baseball, and have at any time scraped acquaintance with the interesting mathematical doctrine of progressive permutations, you will see, when four men equal to a thousand are under the eyes of each other, and of the garrison in the fort, that the whole arsenal of logarithms would give out before you could compute the permutative possibilities of the courage that would be refracted, reflected, compounded and concentrated by all there, each giving courage to and receiving courage from each and all the others. It makes my head ache to think of it. I feel as if I could be brave myself.

Certainly they were that day. To the bitter end of finishing the meal; and they confessed the added courage by gamboling like boys amid awful thunders of the arquebuses, which made a rumble in their time like their successors, the omnibuses, still make to this day on the granite streets of cities populated by deaf folks.

There never was more of a gay, lilting, impudent courage than those four mousquetaires displayed with such splendid coolness and spirit.

But compare it with the fight which Bussy made, single-handed, against the assassins hired by Monsereau and authorized by that effeminate fop, the Due D'Anjou. Of course you remember it. Let me pay you the affectionate compliment of presuming that you have read "La Dame de Monsereau," often translated under the English title, "Chicot, the Jester," that almost incomparable novel of historical romance, by M. Dumas. If, through some accident or even through lack of culture, you have failed to do so, pray do not admit it. Conceal your blemish and remedy the matter at once. At least, seem to deserve respect and confidence, and appear to be a worthy novel-reader if actually you are not. There is a novel that, I assure you on my honor, is as good as the "Three Guardsmen;" but - oh! - so - much - shorter; the pity of it, too! - oh, the pity of it! On the second reading - now, let us speak with frank conservatism - on the second reading of it, I give you my word, man to man, I dreaded to turn every page, because it brought the end nearer. If it had been granted to me to have one wish fulfilled that fine winter night, I should have said with humility: "Beneficent Power, string it out by nine more volumes, presto me here a fresh box of cigars, and the account of your kindness, and my gratitude is closed."

* * * * *

If the publisher of this series did not have such absurd sensitiveness about the value of space and such pitifully small ideas about the nobility of novels, I should like to write at least twenty pages about "Chicot." There are books that none of us ever put down in our lists of great books, and yet which we think more of and delight more in than all the great guns. Not one of the friends I've loved so long and well has been President of the United States, but I wouldn't give one of them for all the Presidents. Just across the hall at this minute I can hear the frightful din of war - shells whistling and moaning, bullets s-e-o-uing, the shrieks of the dying and wounded - Merciful Heaven! the "Don Juan of Asturia" has just blown up in Manila Bay with an awful roar - again! Again, as I'm a living man, just as she has blown up every day, and several times every day, since May 1, 1898. There are two warriors over in the play-room, drenched with imaginary gore, immersed in the tender grace of bestowing chastening death and destruction upon the Spanish foe. Don't I know that they rank somewhat below Admiral Dewey as heroes? But do you suppose that their father would swap them for Admiral Dewey and all the rainbow glories that fine old Yankee sea-dog ever will enjoy - long may he live to enjoy them all! - do you think so? Of course not! You know perfectly well that his - wife - wouldn't - let - him!

I would not wound the susceptibilities of any reader; but speaking for myself - "Chicot" being beloved of my heart - if there was a mean man, living in a mean street, who had the last volume of "Chicot" in existence, I would pour out my library's last heart's blood to get it. He could have all of Scott but "Ivanhoe," all of Dickens but "Copperfield," all of Hugo but "Les Miserables," cords of Fielding, Marryat, Richardson, Reynolds, Eliot, Smollet, a whole ton of German translations - by George! he could leave me a poor old despoiled, destitute and ruined book-owner in things that folks buy in costly bindings for the sake of vanity and the deception of those who also deceive them in turn.

Brother, "Chicot" is a book you lend only to your dearest friend, and then remind him next day that he hasn't sent it back.

*   *   *   *   *

Now, as to Bussy's great fight. He had gone to the house of Madame Diana de Monsereau. I am not au fait upon French social customs, but let us presume his being there was entirely proper, because that excellent lady was glad to see him. He was set upon by her husband, M. de Monsereau, with fifteen hired assassins. Outside, the Due D'Anjou and some others of assassins were in hiding to make sure that Monsereau killed Bussy, and that somebody killed Monsereau! There's a "situation" for you, double-edged treachery against - love and innocence, let us say. Bussy is in the house with Madame. His friend, St. Luc, is with him; also his lacquey and body-physician, the faithful Rely. Bang! the doors are broken in, and the assassins penetrate up the stairway. The brave Bussy confides Diana to St. Luc and Rely, and, hastily throwing up a barricade of tables and chairs near the door of the apartment, draws his sword. Then, ye friends of sudden death and valorous exercise, began a surfeit of joy. Monsereau and his assassins numbered sixteen. In less than three moderate paragraphs Bessy's sword, playing like avenging lightning, had struck fatality to seven. Even then, with every wrist going, he reflected, with sublime calculation: "I can kill five more, because I can fight with all my vigor ten minutes longer!" After that? Bessy could see no further - there spoke fate! - you feel he is to die. Once more the leaping steel point, the shrill death cry, the miraculous parry. The villain, Monsereau, draws his pistol. Bessy, who is fighting half a dozen swordsmen, can even see the cowardly purpose; he watches; he - dodges - the - bullets! - by watching the aim -

"Ye sons of France, behold the glory!"

He thrusts, parries and swings the sword as a falchion. Suddenly a pistol ball snaps the blade off six inches from the hilt. Bessy picks up the blade and in an instant splices - it - to - the - hilt - with - his - handkerchief! Oh, good sword of the good swordsman! it drinks the blood of three more before it - bends - and - loosens - under - the - strain! Bessy is shot in the thigh; Monsereau is upon him; the good Rely, lying almost lifeless from a bullet wound received at the outset, thrusts a rapier to Bessy's grasp with a last effort. Bessy springs upon Monsereau with the great bound of a panther and pins - the - son - of - a - gun - to - the - floor - with - the - rapier - and - watches - him - die!

You can feel faint for joy at that passage for a good dozen readings, if you are appreciative. Poor Bessy, faint from wounds and blood-letting, retreats valiantly to a closet window step by step and drops out, leaving Monsereau spitted, like a black spider, dead on the floor. Here hope and expectation are drawn out in your breast like chewing gum stretched to the last shred of tenuation. At this point I firmly believed that Bessy would escape. I feel sorry for the reader who does not. You just naturally argue that the faithful Rely will surely reach him and rub him with the balsam. That balsam of Dumas! The same that D'Artagnan's mother gave him when he rode away on the yellow horse, and which cured so many heroes hurt to the last gasp. That miraculous balsam, which would make doctors and surgeons sing small today if they had not suppressed it from the materia medica. May be they can silence their consciences by the reflection that they suppressed it to enhance the value and necessity of their own personal services. But let them look at the death rate and shudder. I had confidence in Rely and the balsam, but he could not get there in time. Then, it was forgone that Bessy must die. Like Mercutio, he was too brilliant to live. Depend upon it, these wizards of story tellers know when the knell of fate rings much sooner than we halting readers do.

Bessy drops from the closet window upon an iron fence that surrounded the park and was impaled upon the dreadful pickets! Even then for another moment you can cherish a hope that he may escape after all. Suspended there and growing weaker, he hears footsteps approaching. Is it a rescuing friend? He calls out - and a dagger stroke from the hand of D'Anjou, his Judas master, finds his heart. That's the way Bessy died. No man is proof against the dagger stroke of treachery. Bessy was powerful and the due jealous.

Diana has been carried off safely by the trustworthy St. Luc. She must have died of grief if she had not been kept alive to be the instrument of retributive justice. (In the sequel you will find that this Queen of Hearts descended upon the ignoble due at the proper time like a thousand of brick and took the last trick of justice.)

* * * * *

The extraordinary description of Bussy's fight is beyond everything. You gallop along as if in a whirlwind, and it is only in cooler moments that you discover he killed about twelve rascals with his own good arm. It seems impossible; the scientific, careful readers have been known to declare it impossible and sneer at it with laughter. I trust every novel reader respects scientific folks as he should; but science is not everything. Our scientific friends have contended that the whale did not engulf Jonah; that the sun did not pause over the vale of Askelon; that Baron Munchausen's horse did not hang to the steeple by his bridle; that the beanstalk could not have supported a stout lad like Jack; that General Monk was not sent to Holland in a cage; that Remus and Romulus had not a devoted lady wolf for a step-mother; in fact, that loads of things, of which the most undeniable proof exists in plain print all over the world, never were done or never happened. Bessy was killed, Rely was killed later, Diana died in performing her destiny, St. Luc was killed. Nobody left to make affidavits, except M. Dumas; in his lifetime nobody questioned it; he is now dead and unable to depose; whereupon the scientists sniff scornfully and deny. I hope I shall always continue to respect science in its true offices, but, brethren, are there not times when - science - makes - you - just - a - little - tired?

Heroes! D'Artagnan or Bessy? Choose, good friends, freely; as freely let me have my Bessy.

VIII

HEROINES
A SUBJECT ALMOST WITHOUT AN OBJECT -
WHY THERE ARE FEW HEROINES FOR MEN.

Notwithstanding the subject, there are almost no heroines in novels. There are impossibly good women, absurdly patient and brave women, but few heroines as the convention of worldly thinking demands heroines. There is an endless train of what Thackeray so aptly described as "pale, pious, and pulmonary ladies" who snivel and snuffle and sigh and linger irresolutely under many trials which a little common sense would dissolve; but they are pathological heroines. "Little Nell," "Little Eva," and their married sisters are unquestionable in morals, purpose and faith; but oh! how - they - do - try - the - nerves! How brave and noble was Jennie Deans, but how thick-headed was the dear lass!

These women who are merely good, and enforce it by turning on the faucet of tears, or by old-fashioned obstinacy, or stupidity of purpose, can scarcely be called heroines by the canons of understood definition. On the other hand, the conventions do not permit us to describe as a heroine any lady who has what is nowadays technically called "a past." The very best men in the world find splendid heroism and virtue in

Tess l'Durbeyfield. There is nowhere an honest, strong, good man, full of weakness, though he may be, scarred so much, however with fault, who does not read St. John vii., 3-11, with sympathy, reverence and Amen! The infallible critics can prove to a hair that this passage is an interpolation. An interpolation in that sense means something inserted to deceive or defraud; a forgery. How can you defraud or deceive anybody by the interpolation of pure gold with pure gold? How can that be a forgery which hurts nobody, but gives to everybody more value in the thing uttered? If John vii., 3-11, is an interpolation let us hope Heaven has long ago blessed the interpolator. Does anybody - even the infallible critic - contend that Jesus would not have so said and done if the woman had been brought to Him? Was that not the very flower and savor and soul of His teaching? Would He have said or done otherwise? If the Ten Commandments were lost utterly from among men there would yet remain these four greater:

"Do unto others as ye would they should do unto you."

"Suffer little children to come unto me."

"Go and sin no more."

"Father, forgive them, for they know not what they do."

My lords and ladies, men and women, the Ten Commandments, by the side of these sighs of gentleness, are the Police Court and the Criminal Code, which are intended to pay cruelty off in punishment. These Four are the tears with which sympathy soothes the wounds of suffering. Blessed interpolator of St. John!

There are three marvelous novels in the Bible - not Novels in the sense of fiction, but in the sense of vivid, living narratives of human emotions and of events. A million Novels rest on those nine verses in John, and the nine verses are better than the million books. The story of David and Uriah's wife is in a similar catalogue as regards quality and usefulness; the story of Esther is a pearl of great beauty.

* * * * *

But to return to heroines, let us make a volte face. There is an old story of the lady who wrote rather irritably to Thackeray, asking, curtly, why all the good women he created were fools and the bright women all bad. "The same complaint," he answered, "has been made, Madame, of God and Shakespeare, and as neither has given explanation I can not presume to attempt one." It was curt and severe, and, of course, Thackeray did not write it as it would appear, even though he may have said as much jestingly to some intimate who understood the epigram; but was not the question rather impudently intrusive? Thackeray, you remember, was the "seared cynic" who created Caroline Gann, the gentle, beautiful, glorious "Little Sister," the staunch, pure-hearted woman whose character not even the perfect scoundrelism of Dr. George Brand Firmin could tarnish or disturb. If there are heroines, surely she has her place high amid the noble group!

There are plenty of intelligent persons sacramentally wedded to mere conventions of good and bad. You could never persuade them that Rebecca Sharp - that most perfect daughter of Thackeray's mind - was a heroine. But of course she was. In that world wherein she was cast to live she was indubitably, incomparably, the very best of all the inhabitants to whom you are intimately introduced. Capt. Dobbin? Oh, no, I am not forgetting good Old Dob. Of all the social door mats that ever I wiped my feet upon Old Dob is certainly the cleanest, most patient, serviceable and unrevolutionary. But, just a door mat, with the virtues and attractions of that useful article of furniture - the sublime, immortal prig of all the ages, or you can take the head of any novel-reader under thirty for a football. You may have known many women, from Bernadettes of Massavielle to Borgias of scant neighborhoods, but you know you never knew one who would marry Old Dob, except as that emotional dishrag, Amelia, married him - as the Last Chance on the stretching high-road of uncertain years. No girl ever willingly marries door mats. She just wipes her feet on them and passes on into the drawing room looking for the Prince. It seems to me one of the triumphant proofs of Becky as a heroine that she did not marry Captain Dobbin. She might have done it any day by crooking her little finger at him - but she didn't.

Madame Becky, that smart daughter of an alcoholic gentleman artist and of his lady of the French ballet, inherited the perfect non-moral morality of the artist blood that sang mercurially through her veins. How could she, therefore, how could she, being non-moral, be immoral? It is clear nonsense. But she did possess the instinctive artist morality of unerring taste for selection in choice. Examine the facts meticulously - meticulously - and observe how carefully she selected that best in all that worst she moved among.

In the will I shall some day leave behind me there will be devised, in primogenitural trust forever, the priceless treasure of conviction that Becky was innocent of Lord Steyne. I leave it to any gentleman who has had the great opportunity to look in familiarly upon the outer and upper fringes of the world of unclassed and predatory women and the noble lords that abound thereamong. Let him read over again that famous scene where Becky writes her scorn upon Steyne's forehead in the noble blood of that aristocratic wolf. Then let him give his decision, as an honest juryman upon his oath, whether he is convinced that the most noble Marquis was raging because he was losing a woman, or from the discovery that he was one of two dupes facing each other, and that he was the fool who had paid for both and had had "no run for his money!" Marquises of Steyne do not resent sentimental losses - they can be hurt only in their sportsmanship.

You may begin with the Misses Pinkerton (in whose select school Becky absorbed the intricate hypocrisies and saturated snobbery of the highest English society) and follow her through all the little and big turmoils of her life, meeting on the way of it all the elaborated differentials of the country-gentleman and lady tribe of Crawley, the line officers and bemedalled generals of the army (except honest O'Dowd and his lady), the most noble Marquis and his shadowy and resigned Marchioness, the R - y - l P - rs - n - ge himself - even down to the tuft-hunters Punter and Loder - and if Becky is not superior to every man and woman of them in every personal trait and grace that calls for admiration - then, why, by George! do you take such an interest, such an undying interest, in her? You invariably take the greatest interest in the best character in a story - unless it's too good and gets "sweety" and "sticky" and so sours on your philosophical stomach. You can't possibly take any interest in Dobbin - you just naturally, emphatically, and in the most unreflecting way in the world, say "Oh, d - n Dobbin!" and go right ahead after somebody else. I don't say Becky was all that a perfect Sunday School teacher should have been, but in the group in which she was born to move she smells cleaner than the whole raft of them - to me.

*   *   *   *   *

Thackeray was, next to Shakespeare, the writer most wonderfully combined of instinct and reason that English literature of grace has produced. He has been compared with the Frenchman, Balzac. Since I have no desire to provoke squabbles about favorite authors, let us merely definitely agree that such a comparison is absurd and pass on. Because you must have noticed that Balzac was often feeble in his reason and couldn't make it keep step with his instinct, while in Thackeray they both step together like the Siamese twins. It is a very striking fact, indeed, that during all Becky's intense early experiences with the great world, Thackeray does not make her guilty. All the circumstances of that world were guilty and she is placed amidst the circumstances; but that is all.

"The ladies in the drawing room," said one lady to Thackeray, when "Vanity Fair" in monthly parts publishing had just reached the catastrophe of Rawdon, Rebecca, old Steyne and the bracelet - "The ladies have been discussing Becky Sharpe and they all agree that she was guilty. May I ask if we guessed rightly?"

"I am sure I don't know," replied the "seared cynic," mischievously. "I am only a man and I haven't been able to make up my mind on that point. But if the ladies agree I fear it may be true - you must understand your sex much better than we men!"

That is proof that she was not guilty with Steyne. But straightway then, Thackeray starts out to make her guilty with others. It is so much the more proof of her previous innocence that, incomparable artist as he was in showing human character, he recognized that he could convince the reader of her guilt only by disintegrating her, whipping himself meanwhile into a ceaseless rage of vulgar abuse of her, a thing of which Thackeray was seldom guilty. But it was not really Becky that became guilty - it was the woman that English society and Thackeray remorselessly made of her. I wouldn't be a lawyer for a wagon load of diamonds, but if I had had to be a lawyer I should have preferred to be a solicitor at the London bar in 1817 to write the brief for the respondent in the celebrated divorce case of Crawley vs. Crawley. Against the back-ground of the world she lived in Becky could have been painted as meekly white and beautiful as that lovely old picture of St. Cecilia at the Choir Organ.

Perhaps Becky was not strictly a heroine; but she was a honey.

*   *   *   *   *

Men can not "create" heroines in the sense of shadowing forth what they conceive to be the glory, beauty, courage and splendor of womanly character. It is the indescribable sum of womanhood corresponding to the unutterable name of God. The true man's love of woman is a spirit sense attending upon the actual senses of seeing, hearing, feeling, tasting and smelling. The woman he loves enters into every one of these senses and thus is impounded five-fold upon that union of all of them, which, together with the miracle of mind, composes what we call the human soul as a divine essence. She is attached to every religion, yet enters with authority into none. She is first at its birth, the last to stay weeping at its death. In every great novel a heroine, unnamed, unspoken, undescribed, hovers throughout like an essence. The heroism of woman is her privacy. There is to me no more wonderful, philosophical, psychological and delicate triumph of literary art in existence than the few chapters in "Quo Vadis" in which that great introspective genius, Sienkiewicz, sets forth the growth of the spell of love with which Lygia has encompassed Vinicius, and the singular development and progress of the emotion through which Vinicius is finally immersed in human love of Lygia and in the Christian reverence of her spiritual purity at the same time. It is the miracle of soul in sex.

Every clean-hearted youth that has had the happiness to marry a good woman - and, thank Heaven, clean youths and good women are thick as leaves in Vallambrosa in this sturdy old world of ours - every such youth has had his day of holy conversion, his touch of the wand conferring upon him the miracle of love, and he has been a better and wiser man for it. Not sense love, not the instinctive, restless love of matter for matter, but the love that descends like the dove amid radiance.

*   *   *   *   *

We've all seen that bridal couple; she is as pretty as

peaches; he is as proud of her as if she were a splendid race horse; he glories in knowing she is lovely and accepts the admiration offered to her as a tribute to his own judgment, his own taste and even his merit, which obtained her. There is a certain amount of silliness in her which he soon detects, a touch of helplessness, and unsophistication in knowledge of worldly things that he yet feels is mysteriously guarded against intrusion upon and which makes companionship with her sometimes irksome. He feels superior and uncompensated; from the superb isolation of his greater knowledge, courage and independence, he grants to her a certain tender pity and protection; he admits her faith and purity and - er - but - you see, he is sorry she is not quite the well poised and noble creature he is! Mr. Youngwed is at this time passing through the mental digestive process of feeling his oats. He is all right, though, if he is half as good as he thinks he is. He has not been touched by the live wire of experience - yet; that's all.

Well, in the course of human events, there comes a time when he is frightened to death, then greatly relieved and for a few weeks becomes as proud as if he had actually provided the last census of the United States with most of the material contained in it. A few months later, when the feeble whines and howls have found increased vigor of utterance and more frequency of expression; when they don't know whether Master Jack or Miss Jill has merely a howling spell or is threatened with fatal convulsions; when they don't know whether they want a dog-muzzle or a doctor; when Mr. Youngwed has lost his sleep and his temper, together, and has displayed himself with spectacular effect as a brute, selfish, irritable, helpless, resourceless and conquered - then - then, my dear madame, you have doubtless observed him decrease in self-estimated size like a balloon into which a pin has been introduced, until he looks, in fact, like Master Frog reduced in bulk from the bull-size, to which he aspired, to his original degree.

At that time Mrs. Youngwed is very busy with little Jack or Jill, as the case may be. Her husband's conduct she probably regards with resignation as the first heavy burden of the cross she is expected to bear. She does not reproach him, it is useless; she has perhaps suspected that his assumed superiority would not stand the real strain. But, he is the father of the dear baby and, for that precious darling's sake, she will be patient. I wonder if she feels that way? She has every right to, and, for one, I say that I'll be hanged if I find any fault with her if she does. That is the way she must keep human, and so balance the little open accounts that married folks ought to run between themselves for the purpose of keeping cobwebs and mildew off, or rather of maintaining their lives as a running stream instead of a stagnant pond. A little good talking back now and then is good for wives and married men. Don't be afraid, Mrs. Youngwed; and when the very worst has come, why cry - at - him! One tear weighs more and will hit him harder than an ax. In the lachrymal ducts with which heaven has blessed you, you are more surely protected against the fires of your honest indignation than you are by the fire department against a blaze in the house. And be patient, also; remember, dear sister, that, though you can cry, he has a gift - that - enables - him - to - swear! You and other wedded wives very properly object to swearing, but you will doubtless admit that there is compensation in that when he does swear in his usual good form you - never - feel - any - apprehension - about - the - state -

of - his - health!

This natural outburst of resentment has not lasted three minutes. Mr. Y. has returned to his couch, sulky and ashamed. He pretends to sleep ostentatiously; he - does - not! He is thinking with remarkable intensity and has an eye open. He sees the slender figure in the dim light, hanging over the crib, he hears the crooning, he begins to suspect that there is an alloy in his godlikeness. He looks to earth, listens to the thin, wailing cries, wonders, regrets, wearies, sleeps. At that moment Mrs. Y. should fall on her knees and rejoice. She would if she could leave young Jack or Jill; but she can't - she - never - can. That's what sent Mr. Y. to sleep. It is just as well perhaps that Mrs. Y. is unobservant.

A miracle is happening to Mr. Y. In an hour or two, let us say, there is a new vocal alarm from the crib. Almost with the first suspicion of fretfulness or pain the mother has heard it. Heaven's mysterious telepathy of instinct has operated. Between angels, babies and mothers the distance is no longer than your arm can reach. They understand, feel and hear each other, and are linked in one chain. So, that, when Mr. Y. has struggled laboriously awake and wonders if - that - child - is - going - to - howl - all -. Well, he goes no further. In the dim light he sees again the slender figure hanging over the crib, he hears the crooning and the retreating sobs. It is just as he saw and heard before he fell asleep. No complaints, no reproaches, no irritation. Oh, what a brute he feels! He battles with his reason and his bewilderment. Had he fallen asleep and left her to bear that strain; or has she gone anew to the rescue, while he slept without thought? Up out of his heart the tenderness wells; down into his mind the revelation comes. The miracle works. He looks and listens. In the figure hanging there so patiently and tenderly he sees for the first time the wonderful vision of the sweetheart wife, not lost, but enveloped in the mystery of motherhood; he hears in the crooning voice a tone he never before knew. Mother and child are united in mysterious converse. Where did that girl whom he thought so unsophisticated of the world learn that marvel of acquaintance with that babe, so far removed from his ability to reach? It must be that while he knew the world, she understood the secret of heaven. She is so patient. What a brute he is to grow impatient, when she endures day and night in rapt patience and the joy of content! She can enter a world from which he is barred. And, that is his wife! That was his sweetheart, and is now - ah, what is she? He feels somehow abashed; he knows that if he were ten times better than he is he might still feel unworthy to touch the latchet of her shoes; he feels that reverence and awe have enveloped her, and that the first happy love and longing are springing afresh in his heart. It is his wife and his child; apart from him unless he can note and understand that miracle of nature's secret. Can he? Well, he will try - oh, what a brute! And he watches the bending figure, he hears the blending of soft crooning and retreating sobs - and, listening, he is lost in the wonder and falls under the spell asleep.

Mrs. Y., you are happy henceforth, if you will disregard certain small matters, such as whether chairs or hat-racks are for hats, or whether the marble mantelpiece or the floor is intended for polishing boot heels.

*   *   *   *   *

Of course, such an incident as has been suggested is but one of thousands of golden moments when to the husband comes the sudden dazzling recognition of the mergence of that half-sweetheart, half-mistress, he has admired and a little tired of, into the reverential glory and loveliness of wifehood, motherhood, companion-hood, through all life and on through the eternity of inheritance they shall leave to Jacks and Jills and their little sisters and brothers. In that lies the priceless secret of Christianity and its influence. The unspeakably immoral Greeks reared a temple to Pity; the grossest mythologies of Babylon, Greece, Rome and Carthage could not change human nature. There have been always persons whose temperament made them sympathize with grief and pity the suffering; who, caring none for wealth, had no desire to steal; who purchased a little pleasure for vanity in the thanks received for kindness given. But Christianity saw the jewel underneath the passing emotion and gave it value by cleansing and cutting it. In lust-love is the instinctive secret of the preservation of the race; but the race is not worth preserving that it may be preserved only for lust. Upon that animal foundation is to be built the radiant home of confident, enduring and exchanging love in which all the senses, tastes, hopes, aspirations and delights of friendship, companionship and human society shall find hospitality and comfort. When it has been achieved it is beautiful, a twin to the delicate rose that lies in its own delicious fragrance, happy on the pure bosom of a lovely girl - the rose that is finest and most exquisite because it has sprung from the horrid heat of the compost; but who shall think of the one in the presence of the pure beauty of the other?

Nature and art are entirely unlike each other, though the one simulates the other. The art of beauty in writing, said Balzac, is to be able to construct a palace upon the point of a needle; the art of beauty in living and loving is to build all the beauty of social life and aspiration upon the sordid yet solid and persisting instincts of savagery that lie deep at the bottom of our gross natures.

* * * * *

Now, it is in this tender sacred atmosphere, such as Mr. and Mrs. Youngwed always pass through, that the man worthy of a woman's confidence finds the radiant ideal of his heroine. He may with propriety speak of these transfigured personalities to his intimates or write of them with kindly pleasantry and suggestion as, perhaps, this will be considered. But, there is a monitor within that restrains him from analyzing and describing and dragging into the glare of publicity the sacred details that give to life all its secret happiness, faith and delight. To do so would be ten times worse offense against the ethics of unwritten and unspoken things than describing with pitiless precision the death beds of children, as Little Nell, Paul Dombey, Dora, Little Eva, and, thank heaven! only a few others.

How can anybody bear to read such pages without feeling that he is an intruder where angels should veil their faces as they await the transformation?

"It is not permitted to do evil," says the philosopher, "that good may result."

There are some things that should remain unspoken and undescribed. Have you never listened to some great brute of a sincere preacher of the gospel, as he warned his congregation against the terrible dangers attending the omission of purely theological rites upon infants? Have you thought of the mothers of those children, listening, whose little ones were sick or delicate, and who felt each word of that hard, ominous warning as an agonizing terror? And haven't you wanted to kick the minister out of the pulpit, through the reredos and into the middle of next week? How can anybody harrow up such tender feelings? How can anybody like to believe that a little child will be held to account? Many of us do so believe, perhaps, whether or no; but is it not cruel to shake the rod of terror over us in public? "Suffer little children to come unto Me," said the Master; He did not instruct us to drive them with fear and terror and trembling. Whenever I have heard such sermons I have wanted to get up and stalk out of the church with ostentatiousness of contempt, as if to say to the preacher that his conduct did - not - meet - with - my - approval. But I didn't; the philosopher has his cowardice not less than the preacher.

But there is something meretricious and cheap in the use of material and subjects that lie warm against the very secret heart of nature. The mystery of love and the sanctity of death are to be used by writers and artists only in their ennobling aspect of results. A certain class of French writers have sickened the world by invading the sacredness of passion and giving prostitution the semblance of self-abnegated love; a certain class of English and American writers have purchased popularity by the meretricious parade of the scenes of death-beds. Both are violations of the ethics of art as they are of nature. True love as true sorrow shrinks from exhibition and should be permitted to enjoy the sacredness of privacy. The famous women of the world, Herodias, Semiramis, Aspasia, Thais, Cleopatra, Sapho, Messalina, Marie de Medici,

Catherine of Russia, Elizabeth of England - all of them have been immoral. Publicity to women is like handling to peaches - the bloom comes off, whether or not any other harm occurs. In literature, the great feminine figures, George Sand, Madame de Sevigne, Madame de Stael, George Eliot - all were banned and at least one - the first - was out of the pale. Creative thought has in it the germ of masculinity. Genius in a woman, as we usually describe genius, means masculinity, which, of all things, to real men is abhorrent in woman. True genius in woman is the antithesis of the qualities that make genius in man; so is her heroism, her beauty, her virtue, her destiny and her duty.

Let this be said - even though it be only a jest - one of those smart attempts at epigram, which, ladies, a man has no more power to resist than a baby to resist the desire to improve his thumb by sucking it - that: whenever you find a woman who looks real - that is, who produces upon a real man the impression of being endowed with the splendid gifts for united and patient companionship in marriage - whenever you find her advocating equal suffrage, equal rights, equal independence with men in all things, you may properly run away. Equality means so much, dear sisters. No man can be your equal; you can not be his, without laying down the very jewels of the womanliness that men love. Be thankful you have not this strength and daring; he possesses those in order that he many stand between you and more powerful brutes. Now, let us try for a smart epigram: But no! hang the epigram, let it go. This, however, may be said: That, whenever you find a woman wanting all rights with man; wanting his morals to be judged by hers, or willing to throw hers in with his, or itching to enter his employments and labors and willing that he shall - of course - nurse the children and patch the small trousers and dresses, depend upon it that some weak and timid man has been neglecting the old manly, savage duty of applying quiet home murder as society approves now and then.

www.ingramcontent.com/pod-product-compliance
Lightning Source LLC
Chambersburg PA
CBHW032013040426
42448CB00006B/614